IN
THE
WIND

Sensing the Nearness of God in
the Ordinary Moments of Life

Dr. Billy Burch

Copyright © 2023 by Dr. Billy Burch

In the Wind

Sensing the Nearness of God in the Ordinary Moments of Life

Unless otherwise indicated, all Scripture quotations are taken from the Holy Bible, New Living Translation, copyright 1996, 2004, 2015 by Tyndale House Foundation. Used by permission of Tyndale of Tyndale House Publishers, Carol Stream, Illinois 60188. All rights reserved.

Scripture taken from the New King James Version®. Copyright © 1982 by Thomas Nelson. Used by permission. All rights reserved.

All rights reserved. No part of this publication may be reproduced, distributed or transmitted in any form or by any means, including photocopying, recording, or other electronic or mechanical methods, without the prior written permission of the publisher, except in the case of brief quotations embodied in critical reviews and certain other noncommercial uses permitted by copyright law.

Although the author and publisher have made every effort to ensure that the information in this book was correct at press time, the author and publisher do not assume and hereby disclaim any liability to any party for any loss, damage, or disruption caused by errors or omissions, whether such errors or omissions result from negligence, accident, or any other cause.

Adherence to all applicable laws and regulations, including international, federal, state and local governing professional licensing, business practices, advertising, and all other aspects of doing business in the US, Canada or any other jurisdiction is the sole responsibility of the reader and consumer.

Neither the author nor the publisher assumes any responsibility or liability whatsoever on behalf of the consumer or reader of this material. Any perceived slight of any individual or organization is purely unintentional.

The resources in this book are provided for informational purposes only and should not be used to replace the specialized training and professional judgment of a health care or mental health care professional.

Neither the author nor the publisher can be held responsible for the use of the information provided within this book. Please always consult a trained professional before making any decision regarding treatment of yourself or others.

ISBN: 979-8-89109-413-0 - ebook
ISBN: 979-8-89109-412-3 - paperback
ISBN: 979-8-89109-535-9 - hardcover

This book is dedicated to Kimberly...

My beautiful bride;

My biggest fan;

My constant encourager;

My godly example;

My lifelong friend;

My soulmate;

My love.

Don't forget your free reflection journal which will inspire you to internalize each chapter of *In the Wind*. This downloadable and printable journal provides helpful reflection exercises which will enable you to lean into the powerful insights of *In the Wind*. To access your free reflection journal, visit billyburch.com.

TABLE OF CONTENTS

BEGINNINGS 1

MYSTERY 17

BELIEF 33

WONDER 51

PURPOSE 69

EMPTINESS 85

PAIN 103

REMORSE 121

BLESSING 137

LIGHT 153

LOVE 169

FINDINGS 183

ACKNOWLEDGEMENTS 199

ABOUT THE AUTHOR. 203

BEGINNINGS

"*Every sunset is an opportunity to reset. Every sunrise begins with new eyes.*"
— *Richie Norton*

"*Every moment is a fresh beginning.*"
— *T.S. Eliot*

A renewed interest in habits, particularly morning habits, has resurfaced in the self-help world within the last few years. The idea that forming new habits can bring success and transformation is not a new concept, but regardless, it has caught the public consciousness. I think for most people, achieving more, reigning life in, and moving toward a goal has immense appeal. It does for me. No one wants to stagnate.

Textbooks say that anything, left to itself, will move from a place of order to disorder and, therefore, will have a propensity to decline in energy as well—they call this "entropy." And it sounds like my office. And a lot like my life.

IN THE WIND

But we aren't left to ourselves, at least we don't have to be. External forces can be applied which will dynamically change the internal characteristics so as to hold off entropy, even reverse it. Take for instance a need to keep water boiling. You have a dozen friends arriving for pasta in a half hour. The pasta requires boiling water to soften the hardened sticks of spaghetti into the perfect texture, ready to accept the homemade tomato and meat sauce which has been simmering on the other burner, wafting through the apartment for the last eight hours. So everything must stay hot. Room temperature will not be enough to prepare this meal. Simple enough: keep the power on the stove set at high, and keep the pot touching the burner. While entropy makes its best effort to cool the water to its normal room temperature, the heat from the spiral stove filaments wins the day. Problem solved.

In order to truly reach our potential, experience real joy, recover from damaging patterns– in essence, to become the best person I can be, a power from the outside must be allowed to make its way inside. Habits will help. Routines will prove valuable. But will those be able to support you when you are at your lowest point in life, with seemingly nowhere to turn, no strength to keep going? And what about when entropy proves a bit stronger this month than it was last month? Is it really only a matter of reading *another* book about how to spend your morning?

Please don't misunderstand. I am a proponent of books that help me establish better ways to live, love, think, and work—after all, I wrote one. But I am also convinced that something far deeper needs to happen within. Something of substance, something of a foundation on which I can build my life. This something will need to have enough power to supply strength, enough wisdom to give direction, and enough consistency to always be there, to meet and tend to me at my very worst.

Belief in something bigger presupposes something grand and hopeful: a reason. Reason answers *why*.

I've asked my fair share of why's, which all too often leaned on the unfavorable and cynical side of things. A few years ago, I rode the elevator to the third floor of Children's Hospital to visit a young teenage boy with intestinal problems whom I knew. Turns out he would be fine, but that was not the case for the patient sharing a room with him. This boy was curled up in a ball, lying in what looked like an oversized crib. I was shocked to learn of his age—he was fourteen, the same age as the boy I was visiting, though he looked no larger than a five year old. A profound sadness welled up in me. Certainly not because I felt this young man to hold any less value than any other human—all human life holds an intrinsic value based on humanness, not on size, intellect, skill, or future prospect. It's just that that kind of life is not what I would wish for anyone. I walked from that room, followed the polished linoleum tile back to the elevator, pressed "Ground Floor," and asked, "Why?"

We humans feel the need to make sense of things, to know that a bigger purpose exists. The more we know about the "reasons" behind any given situation, the more we feel justified in making a judgment call as to whether it was good or bad. Here's the problem: we don't know all the possible outcomes given differing possibilities. Our finite minds can only grasp one thing at a time—we can weave together a few more to create a narrative of sorts, but we have no ability to arrange all the pieces of fabric and colors of thread to make complete sense of any situation on our own. So we ask "why," in hopes that an answer will come, all the while knowing that the full answer to that question is well out of our reach.

Then there are the why's which catapult people into careers as great scientists, inventors, engineers, chefs, coaches, teachers. When we ask why one pinch of salt is better than three, why more air pressure might be helpful to a new flight design, why an antibody interacts with blood cells and fights sickness, or why throwing a four-seam rather than two-seam fastball generates more speed, we are propelled into better and more efficient ways of doing things. These are good and helpful things. To have a reason for anything, whether an event or object, good or bad, brings us to a beginning and end all at the same time. X caused Y. And simply put, Y makes sense. Therefore, so does X.

But it goes far deeper than that. There are bigger questions out there, like, "is there a reason for me?" It's a valid question. And if there is a reason for me, what is it? And who holds that information? The mere thought projects our minds upward and outward. Someone out there knows.

There is a reason for the trees which line the lakefront shores, a reason for the water and the frogs jumping in the shallows. There is a reason for the sound of children splashing and for the beauty of the sun reflecting off the ripples of tiny waves. There is a reason for the birds migrating south from colder places and for raccoons prying the lids off garbage cans. There is a reason for the events of our lives which teach us big things and grow our little minds, and this reason lies in a realm beyond our understanding.

The premise of this book is that God, that someone out there who is bigger than us, desires to be known. He has no interest in being covert, irrelevant, or unknown. We sense something more, and for good reason. There is just too much evidence to not sense it, however inexplicable that sense may be. So God, generally speaking, displays His creativity to everyone, making the transcendent tangible, the impossible reachable. Specifically, however, He notices *you*. Generally, He spreads a blanket of goodness over the whole earth. Specifically, He loves you.

I sat quietly on a small watercraft in the Chincoteague Bay under blue skies and a bright sun. A northeasterly wind kicked up at about two o'clock, stirring the waters and agitating the waves. The bay became unwieldy. Waves began rolling over the craft as I rose and plummeted with each one. I had to do something. Just sitting there was not an option. Given the conditions, I decided it best to ride back to the harbor.

The wind tells us things. It tells us that something is coming, whether a storm or a high-pressure weather pattern that blows away the humidity, perfect for an evening picnic. Wind also stirs things, directing our attention to what is right in front of us. God does the same thing. He brings winds that stir us in a deep place, making us aware of His presence, and winds which speak to us, reminding us that something more is on its way.

I believe in God. Which is to say, I believe God exists. "In the beginning, God...", a famous beginning if there ever was one. We must start there. As far as starting points, that is a good one. The existence of something beyond ourselves is always a good starting point because it means the world cannot and must not revolve around me. That is a certain way to make a mess of things. God, however, in spite of our flaws and predispositions, considers us immensely valuable. I believe God is near and involved, interacting with us, noticing us, tending to our delicate and harsh emotions.

I find something bewildering. At some point or another, everyone blames God. Often people who spend their lives denying a higher power are the same people who blame God. When a friend loses their job, God is blamed. When a pulled trigger kills an innocent bystander, God is blamed. When an incurable disease affects your neighbor's daughter, God is blamed. How often do you hear people (or even yourself) say, "With so much evil and pain in the world, how can there be a god?"

I understand. I've done my fair share of blaming God. The buck has to stop somewhere.

IN THE WIND

Walking into the elevator in the hospital after having seen that little boy, a tiny beep sounded, telling me that the doors were about to close and that my visit was officially over. As the elevator carried me downward to the ground level, I remember saying to God, "God, wherever you are, please listen because I am struggling. I am having a hard time understanding the goodness of your plan in all of that." We've all asked similar questions. Experiences like that tend to isolate the pain that goes along with living life and shade us from the immense volume of good that permeates all of life.

So I have a better question: "With so much good in the world, how can there *not* be a god?" Worth thinking through.

Two months ago on a late weeknight, I walked along a busy street in a small town in Bosnia when a sound of clicking flew into my ear like a runaway gnat. The tempo and volume of the clicking both increased, indicating something was gaining on me.

I turned. A stray dog, speckled white with large brown spots, closed in on my heels. I thought it was chasing me—which is always my immediate thought, whenever an unleashed dog approaches me with such speed and intentionality of eye contact. I froze. No fight or flight—I just froze. Then the dog, in one great movement and with all the strength it could muster...sat at my feet.

I inhaled and exhaled and let my shoulders rest for a moment in a slump. "And who are you?" I asked. From that moment on, we were friends.

When I walked, the dog scooted along right next to me. When I stopped, the dog sat at my feet. And there we were, me and my new, shaggy, brown-and-white spotted companion. Strangely, it kept a keen eye on my feet, which I'm pretty sure resembled one of its tasty dog bones. Occasionally, the dog would dart from its position and chase a passing car so as to attempt to take a bite of the rear fender. Each time I thought, "Well, I'll be burying a dog tonight." But each time, it escaped unscathed.

As I walked into a late night cafe, the dog pranced away, looking for another pedestrian it might temporarily befriend. I sat over a cup of cappuccino and, as I stirred in an extra packet of sugar, looked out the rain-speckled window and thought about the dog's strange behavior and spotted fur. I realized it was probably a herding dog. I had seen herding dogs in action on a farm one hot, summer day at a sheep-shearing festival. Amazing creatures—and each of them spotted. It all made total sense now—from its interest in ankles and moving cars to its shape, size, and skill, all the evidence pointed to a breed which thrives on rounding up moving and living things.

The point is, there is no changing the desires, cravings, and natural abilities which lived deep inside that dog. We call that instinct.

Pigeons return to the same cage after hundreds of hours of flight. Mares lick their colts clean after biting away the umbilical cord. Goats use their horns to shove their suckling kids to nourishment. Owls triangulate in the forest with their hooting. Busy bees serve the queen. Instinct is real, powerful, and confounding.

I believe we humans have instinct as well. Survival, defense, food gathering, and reproduction are, on one hand, obvious instincts. Propensity toward a certain discipline—such as math, art, music, literature, engineering, or rounding up screaming kids at a summer camp—is, I believe, another instinct. Some relegate these natural inclinations to genetics, some to a calling. Whatever you call it, something inside us undeniably draws us toward one thing or another. It is why colleges offer so many majors to try to meet people in their proclivity. Trades abound for these various predispositions. I will also call this instinct. This instinct, I believe, comes close to describing one more familiarity which resides in all of us: an awareness of God.

BEGINNINGS

I recently struck up a conversation with a service representative at an auto dealer. He was obviously distraught, so I asked if everything was OK. He quickly responded yes, then after a moment, changed his mind and told me of a coworker who may not make it through the night after a truck smashed into her car the evening before. I told him I would pray for her and would ask others to do the same. We then engaged in small talk about God, church, and faith. He responded with something I have heard time and again over the last few years: "I am not religious, but I am very spiritual."

I knew what that phrase meant—and it goes right back to instinct. Within us lies an undeniable sense that spirituality is not just theological rhetoric. It's real.

People who use that phrase genuinely sense the spiritual void within them. They have an awareness of "God," but a dissonant note of resistance floats through the chorus. Most non-religious-but-spiritual people reside in one of several camps: there are those who are unwilling to submit to a higher authority which holds them accountable for their actions; those who mistrust religion and religious institutions; those who struggle with a great confusion over which religion is the right religion, and so on. For whatever reason, instead of leaning into this sense of inherent spirituality, they avoid it, like walking away from a restaurant after reading concerning comments on Yelp. They, or someone they know, likely experienced something distressing enough about religion to make them keep their distance. And now, like walking through midsummer briars when there's an easy trail nearby, it's just not worth the pain of pushing through.

So what do we do with this sense of the supernatural, the spiritual? Why do we have this instinct inside of us to seek (or return back to) God? How do we wrestle with this inclination toward God? Those are the questions of this book. If God desires to be known, which I believe he does, then those questions ought to be as practical and pertinent as asking for the time.

For most, finding God is a journey. Many begin this journey with questions which are prompted by an acute awareness of divine intrusion into everyday life. This journey, like most journeys, takes energy and time and emotional expenditure. It takes the courage to risk, the ability to persevere, and a willingness to face fears. Even so, it is a journey that ought to be taken to its very end.

Much like a rollercoaster.

I don't know if I like rollercoasters. I sit in a seat where I can't escape in order to take a journey

I can't control. The cars begin a slow ascent. The clickety-clacking breeds a type of consternation, or downright dread, as the cars arrive at the crest of the rollercoaster only to disappear in a free-fall. Downward momentum, twists, turns, and loops lead us to an abrupt stop on the wooden platform. The safety harness lifts to verify that the ride is finally over. Fellow passengers make eye contact with each other, smiling, gasping, laughing, stumbling and then, somehow, wanting to do it all over again.

A rollercoaster is a bit like life— the excitement, the panic, the dread, the slow climb, the speedy descent, the twists and turns, the screams...and then, to our surprise, a craving for more. "More" being the operative word, because it points to something further, higher, something beyond us. A rollercoaster is never enough. Life through our five senses is not enough. We always want *more*.

Sensing the supernatural begins a journey, a search. That search, like it or not, is unavoidable. We are hardwired for it.

This hardwiring is a sense, an instinct, a supernatural awareness, and what could best be described as a "haunting."

When I was a child, the other neighborhood kids and I would go sledding at the old church every time we had a snow day. In all our excitement, none of us remembered—until we arrived and saw the church's cornerstone, etched with the year 1715—the *risk* of sledding here. Close to the sledding hill was the graveyard, with its oldest headstone dating back to 1689. That meant one thing: ghosts.

Sledding at the old church was risky, but not due to snow, ice, and the road at the bottom of the hill. It was risky because we might be seen by a ghost. Once a ghost sees you, as all children know, they don't forget. This was most markedly felt while packing up and leaving the churchyard. One day, we all swore we saw a figure in the gable window.

Those types of inexplicable senses point to a greater constant. We live with the knowledge that something bigger and beyond the physical world is both out there and near, transcendent and immanent, distant yet involved in our affairs. It is a haunting—not the pale, ghostly-type haunting, but a haunting as in the objective sense. Haunting can be described as a seen or unseen event—heard or unheard, tactile or non-tactile—where something is sensed. One or the other of our senses will pick up at least a portion of a haunting. We just might not be able to describe it precisely. The thing about haunting, though, is this: you can't get away from it. The sense is real.

The sense we children got of something otherworldly in that graveyard is similar to the sense we humans get of God existing. It's a feeling that leads us to a conclusion that something else is out there, maybe not so scary as a ghost, but nevertheless something real and intriguing.

God is drawing you in many ways—some of which you can explain, some of which you cannot. When you become aware of this "haunting" and begin to float the idea of God's nearness, taking a moment to contemplate, ponder, and let the current take you where it may, you can be sure that some interesting things will happen deep within you. For in those moments, you know that God is making you more aware of him today than you were yesterday.

Maybe you are sensing the stirrings, hauntings, or instinctual draw to God. Pursue them. There is no greater joy, contentment, and confidence getting through life than to realize that God notices *you*. He is getting your attention. He has more for you. There are things in your past he wants to heal. Things in your future to know and do. God wants to fill your life with love, goodness, freedom. To know God is to know these.

You chose to read this book because you, too, have experienced this sense of supernatural involvement. Maybe it surprised you. I find there is an increasing wave of people who are disenchanted with the effect of secularism. Take God out, take the spiritual out, and you have taken away a core aspect of who you are. We are mental, physical, emotional, social, and *spiritual* beings. We cease to be whole if we extract one. Once you realize something of this magnitude is missing in your soul, the nagging sense won't go away. Because it can't.

    I have talked to many people in my lifetime about God, or a higher power, or a spiritual entity. I noticed similarities in the way God interacts with and "speaks to" people. The rest of this book suggests ten of these. One or more *will* knock on your door—odds are, they already have. Some of you will welcome these knocks; some of you won't. But whether you welcome them or not, ignoring the knocking is not an option. The one knocking is very patient and willing to knock for as long as it takes, waiting on your porch in hopes that you proceed closer to the door and, upon opening it, closer to the wholeness and newness which God offers.

MYSTERY

"The world, even the smallest parts of it, is filled with things you don't know."

Sherman Alexie

"Let my heart be still a moment and this mystery explore..."

Edgar Allan Poe

The Atlantic beaches, which are only a few hours away from me, seem to call me incessantly. The ocean is always lapping its waves upon the shores of my mind. Having packed, fueled and driven a few hours, I'm satisfied only when I'm there, breathing in the thick salt air.

One evening, only a mere twenty minutes' drive away from my family beach destination, a somewhat alarming sight caught my eye. Red and white lights in the distance—50, maybe more—dotted the landscape, flashing and intermingling. With the sun crouched behind the treeline, my depth perception failed—but whatever it was, it was big. I assumed a major car crash, a fire, a natural disaster summoning emergency vehicles from dozens of stations. I drove closer, my heart rate slightly increased. I slowed. But no crash, no disaster. As a matter of fact, there were no emergency vehicles at all. No sirens, no spotlights. Only red and white blinking lights with no observable cadence, like a swarm of giant fireflies.

A small sign stood alongside this two-lane road, nestled between a chainlink fence and the bay. It read: NASA. An overwhelming sense ran through me as I read the sign. I tried to discern the feeling, being somewhere on a fine line between palpable excitement and a trace of fear. A shiver went through my spine. I pulled over. The red lights dotted the tops of an air traffic control tower, multiple radio towers, and a dozen mammoth radars which pointed in all directions. The largest radar, standing about six stories high, pointed directly up, resembling a giant champagne glass.

The fact is, the whole complex is a communication device, a giant receiver. The information it gathers is, I'm sure, stockpiled in a hard drive somewhere deep in the earth so no one will make a documentary about what goes on far in the blackness of the night, beyond the sparkling starlight. What's really out there? NASA knows, and perhaps they won't tell us for fear of causing widespread panic. I wonder, is what lies out there fairly mundane? Are interstellar activities so routine, like working a nine-to-five job where everyone is looking at the clock? Or do the stars hold so fantastic a secret as would incite frenzy, like an air raid siren in the early morning? Let's be honest, the information NASA gathers—even including that which is not shared with the public—is only a fraction of what could be known, a cell wall compared to the Great Wall, the moon compared to the Milky Way.

The thought produces mystery.

Mystery arrives at the doorstep of our minds whenever we encounter people, places, or experiences which ask questions to which there are no reasonable answers. A mystery doesn't mean there isn't an answer, just that I don't have it. But someone does, somewhere, which is exactly what makes it a mystery. There is an answer to the mystery of the Lost Colony on the shores of North Carolina in the late 16th century.

There is an answer to why a plane goes missing in the south Pacific, never to be found again. There is an answer for the late night screeches in an old

Civil War battlefield in Pennsylvania. I don't know the answer. But someone does.

People are naturally drawn to stories, and when a story combines with something unknown—a conspiracy, or a legend, or supernatural involvement—our curiosity shifts into overdrive. A mystery is born.

Documentaries mesmerize us for that very reason. We watch them in hopes of discovering something which is largely unknown to most. The process of discovery, however, intrigues the viewer even when there is no definitive outcome. That is when mystery kicks in. We want to know, but we don't know, yet something inside of us is drawn to the mysterious.

Uncertainty breeds curiosity. Curiosity stimulates questioning and research. The more research, the more discovery, the more fascination, and before you know it, the hope for more revelation has blossomed. Even so, sometimes this cyclical process produces little in terms of concrete knowledge. Hence, theories develop and mysteries expand. Think Area 51.

Mystery, on one hand, says to us, "There is something more. More to know. More to see. More out there than my finite mind can comprehend." On the other hand, mystery says to us, "Someone knows." The intersection between sensory data (what we know through our five senses), and this feeling of incompleteness generates mystery. When reading Sir Arthur Conan Doyle, or Janet Evanovich, you see and hear and feel the events and actions on the page. The clues move you toward a resolution. But those clues are inadequate to solve the puzzle because they are incomplete. There's just too much space between the clues. Now you have a mystery. There is more to the story, I just don't know it—yet.

Intrigue and a draw toward the eerie and eccentric have always captivated humans. From campfire stories in caves thousands of years ago to television screens today, strange and ghostly stories have always had the power to keep a shaking, wide-eyed, twelve-year-old intrigued. Someone tells a story sending chills down your forearm, but when they stop, you tell them to keep going. That is the power of mystery.

Mysteries don't all have to be scary, however. I have heard stories where the wreckage from an auto accident found at the bottom of the cliff formed the shape of a hand when found, and everyone walked away unscathed; where a bright light caused people to run out of a propane-filled house before the explosion; where a canopy shielded soldiers from fiery napalm dropped from an enemy jet in Vietnam—no one was even singed; where people saw angels, or demons, or ghostly figures, or heard heavenly music, or even familiar voices. Mystery, then, creates a space in our minds for things out there which we just don't fully understand.

Every culture, in some way or another, gets sucked into the vortex of the mysterious and otherworldly. Whether the ancient Greeks or the wise Native Americans; whether the multifaceted ancient Egyptians of the Nile or the Aztecs of Tenochtitlan; whether the Hebrews under Moses or the Romans under Pontius Pilate, they had a name for this: God. Or gods. Either way, the peoples of these great civilizations were all aware of something more out there brought forth by the mystery of otherworldliness. At the very least, something bigger than us exists.

Long ago, there came upon the scene of human being's grand meta-story a figure, a man among the many millions who have, up to that point, walked upon earth's surface. This man was called a Mystery. So mysterious was he that the entire way by which we count years today revolves around the time of his birth over 2000 years ago. Jesus, this mystery man, caught the attention of the civilized world.

He was described by one of his followers as "God's mysterious plan, which is Christ himself. In him lie hidden all the treasures of wisdom and knowledge" (Col. 2:2-3). Interesting. Mention hidden treasures and I am immediately hooked. Throw in hidden wisdom and knowledge for good measure and I think we have the makings of something *very* alluring.

Here is a person, Christ (used as a "title" for Jesus, which means "Messiah", the prophesied savior of the Jewish nation), who is said to be God's plan—a mysterious plan, wrapped up in the unknowable mind of God. The parts of God's mind knowable to us are only so because God chose to reveal them. We, then, can and do know things about God, and nature, and the human psyche, and love, and kindness, and science. We, too, know about this mysterious figure in history named Jesus because God chose to reveal him to us.

An event or experience or puzzle is a *mystery* precisely because there is a fragment of it which remains completely hidden. The full answer to one or all questions surrounding a particular mystery escapes us. Moreover, according to that passage, there is a "hiddenness" in this person of Jesus. The passage in Paul's letter to the people of Colossae said that all the treasures of wisdom and knowledge are hidden inside of Jesus. Stop and ponder the magnitude of that treasure. Who would not want even a sliver of that kind of wisdom and knowledge? But the verse above says that in him lies *all* of it. A great mystery indeed. And if that is so, then someone does know how everything works—that person is just not me.

That same letter also said that this mysterious man of history "was kept secret for centuries and generations past, but now it has been revealed..." (Col. 1:26) So here is a captivating thought: God wants to be known. And that being true, he picked the appointed time and place to make himself known. And now we know more of God because this mystery of Jesus has been revealed. Again, interesting.

Mystery has a symbiotic relationship with hiddenness. We find examples of these interdependent relationships in nature. For example, underwater photographs of sharks often reveal a dozen or so zebra-colored fish swimming alongside them. Sharks have established an unlikely association with this species of pilot fish. The pilot fish learned long ago to eat parasites off the shark's skin and even between sharks teeth, as risky as that sounds. But that risk has paid off. Predators now generally avoid pilot fish because of their big friend.

MYSTERY

The question is, did the shark find the pilot fish? Or did the pilot fish find their shark? Hard to tell. It's called symbiosis—it works well for both of them.

Back to our subject. Mystery feeds off of hiddenness. Hiddenness has a prominent place alongside mystery. All of that draws us in and propels us to search, sift, and find out more.

My brother, sister, and I used to hunt for fossils when we were children and believe it or not, enjoyed relative success. On a lesser-known mountain in West Virginia, where the Back Creek led to much greater waters, small clay-like stones formed a natural walkway along the running brook. These rocks, easily broken in half upon dashing them onto the ground or hitting them with other larger and harder rocks, would often contain the form of a long-gone living creature. Anticipation grew as we held each rock in our little hands. Would we strike it rich, or toss it in the water and choose another? There would be that one rock, however, which carefully opened to reveal the shape of a shrimp-like crustacean. And we would study it and ask questions and take in the mystery of it all. How did a shrimp get to the top of this mountain, when we are nowhere near the coast? And how did it get in that rock?

Our lives are a succession of finding rocks. We pick one rock among the choices of rocks in front of us. We open it, and most of the time the contents within are fairly uneventful. But once in a while, the mystery appears and we stop, feel, ask, search. We want answers. And God desires to be known. When those two intersect, something mysterious (and miraculous) happens. This must not be lost on us.

One day, at the time when the sun began its trek back toward the horizon, Jesus sponged the dust and sweat off his forehead with the fringe of his robe and settled onto a land perch near Lake Gennesaret. Exhausted from days of crowds who clamored for his attention—the crippled who needed healing, the ill who needed recovery, the lame who needed to walk, the blind who needed to see, the brokenhearted who needed mending—Jesus caught some much-needed alone time. Though he loved every one of those he encountered, even he needed rejuvenation.

But the crowds were intrigued by this mystery man, and to some, he was their only hope. Scattering about along the lake shores, they eventually found him. Upon seeing the crowd, Jesus had compassion and reminded himself that they were like sheep without a shepherd. So he stood on a boat anchored just beyond the shoreline to do one of the things he did best: teach.

Jesus wanted the crowds to understand more about the love of God, love for each other, the immense grace and compassion God has for everyone, and ultimately hope. But he also desired to impart to them a reason as to why they felt this intrigue every time he spoke. (Jesus, by the way, is still seen by most people around the world as one of the greatest teachers that ever lived.)

To do so, he told a story.

Jesus often crafted short, well-told stories to handle the heavy lifting of much of his teaching—for good reason. Stories are not often forgotten in the same way facts may be. Matthew, one of Jesus's twelve disciples, records that he never spoke without using such teaching aids as illustrations, fables, parables, and stories. Such manner of teaching was to be expected from Jesus, as was predicted of him in the Psalms hundreds of years before: "I will speak to you in parables. I will explain things hidden since the creation of the world" (Ps. 78:2). These hidden things held tremendous meaning and value to the crowds once revealed. In order to express concepts of such significance and force, Jesus turned to the arts (storytelling), for arts were created for expression and were meant to reach a deeper place within us.

For instance, on one occasion Jesus wanted to make a point about the goodness of God spreading quickly throughout the land, the growth of which is often unnoticed. He clearly could have just stated the point: "The goodness of God spreads quickly, and is often unnoticed," and then moved to another subject. Instead, Jesus used a short story to illustrate the point: "The Kingdom of Heaven is like the yeast a woman used in making bread. Even though she put only a little yeast in three measures of flour, it permeated every part of the dough" (Matt. 13:33). Universally understood and instantly memorable, the parable describes the rising dough which has multiplied from such a small quantity of yeast, secretly and quietly. Before you know it, it's done.

On another occasion, Jesus saw a need for the multitudes to clearly understand the passionate, constant, and unwavering love of God for all people. Instead of stating the facts, he showed them by telling a short story: "Or suppose a woman has ten silver coins and loses one. Won't she light a lamp and sweep the entire house and search carefully until she finds it? And when she finds it, she will call in her friends and neighbors and say, 'Rejoice with me because I have found my lost coin'" (Luke

15:8-10). Yes! That's it! When God loses one precious coin out of the ten he has in his leather bag, he searches deep into the night, moving the furniture, sweeping every corner until he sees the glint of silver off the flickering flame of the lamp. Then, he gingerly takes it between his thumb and forefinger, smiling, and joyfully tells everyone that he has found his cherished coin. In essence, Jesus implored, "That's what God thinks of all of you!"

In the way of unforgettable little stories like these, Jesus's teaching burrowed its way to a deeper place. Stories do that. They make us ask questions as we compare ourselves to each character and situation. It is an art form, and, again, art was meant to affect a pensive, personal place deep within.

After one particular teaching, Jesus's disciples asked him why he always used stories to teach. Jesus answered simply and strangely: "to those who listen to my teaching, more understanding will be given. But for those who are not listening, even what little understanding they have will be taken away from them" (Matt. 13:12). But why is this the case? "For they look, but they don't really see. They hear, but they don't really listen or understand" (Matt. 13:13). And what is he really saying? He is saying, don't let the opportunity for mystery to sink in pass you by.

When someone is described as being "sharp of mind," it means they really listen to what they hear, think about what they see, and respond appropriately. The word "sharp" came to be used because a "cutting edge" intellect was one defined by precision. Being sharp means to be keen, aware, eager, and wise. In other words, to be sharp is part of what it means to be the best "you." A dull shovel won't cut through the dirt and roots. A dull knife only rips the filet. Those utensils are not living up to their potential—but they could, if they are sharpened.

We must let awareness, eagerness, and wisdom take us to its end when we sense the mysterious. Let intellectual pursuit and precision lead the way. Be sharp—aware, keen. You may not know all the answers. Mystery is like that. But Someone knows. We come to a place of wisdom when we understand (or at least admit, whether we understand or not) that God has something to do with the intersection of the mystery of the supernatural and the reality of the here and now.

I find myself chuckling a bit when something inside me demands that I should be able to know everything about all the things affecting me at this given moment in time. If I knew all possibilities and could solve all mysteries, God would cease to be God, because I would take that place. Laughable, for sure.

When I get frustrated that I don't have all the answers, I remind myself that God is God, and in spite of my lack of understanding, new possibilities await. Accepting this fact is the first step to inviting the beautiful mystery of God into our here and now, into the present moment, and into the realization that God has more for you.

Let mystery take you to that place.

BELIEF

"Reality is that which, when you stop believing in it, it doesn't go away."

Philip Dick

"I believe that deep inside us we all strive to move forward and up, to scale new heights."

Paul Stoltz, Erik Weihemeyer

As a child, I spent many a December night staring at the crackled red paint on the bulb which lit my bedroom window. The curtains didn't quite touch, allowing me to peek through at the red glow reflecting off the fingerprinted window and worn white panes. We lacked resources for the extensive Christmas decorations, like the lights which lit some of the other houses in the neighborhood. But that never stopped us from the excitement of decorating—including an electric candle in every window. It was Christmastime and I loved every bit of it.

Parades of cars drove by to see the grandeur and glamorous magic of the fantastically decorated houses down the street—it became a yearly tradition for many families. Meanwhile, the entirety of our decorations fit into three mid-sized cardboard boxes, stored for eleven months out of the year in the far side of the attic. Every year those boxes came down carefully through an opening in the ceiling, the rickety folding steps barely holding together for yet another year. The decorations seen from the outside amounted mostly to those white plastic candles, now an aged ivory, set in every front-facing window in our one-story house.

The modest light created a Christmastime warmth, gently reminding us of the special season—like the slightly smokey taste from hardened white icing on the gingerbread house given to us by the neighbor every year. She was never without a cigarette. From the outside, the glow through the windows changed the whole character of our old brick house, making it seem much more alive and inviting. Even more intense was the transformation felt on the inside.

Every year I would test the box of bulbs to determine which ones still lit when screwed into the candles. Bulbs age, too. Years of storage in the attic's extreme heat and cold and the shuffling of boxes caused the loose bulbs to roll around, cracking the perfect coat of red, or green, or blue, or orange. But that never seemed to bother us. Maybe it gave the little bulbs character, and maybe it made the new bulbs seem that much more special with their glossy coat of paint.

It seems to me that years age us in much the same way. The more the years go by—the more shuffling from here to there, the more highs and lows—the more the cracks appear. The more cracks that appear, the more that something else surfaces: the need for a reason to believe in something big. Really big.

When I was about twelve years old, staring at the peeling green lightbulb in my window, it occurred to me that, year after year, these same lights come down from the attic in the beginning of December. There must be something to this, a reason for the constancy, a reason for the season. Something big. Something real.

And on this night, while staring at the bulb, I noticed something else: moving specks, reflections, and a pink hue, all dancing together right outside my window. *Snow!* A lot of it! Maybe it would be a white Christmas after all! And more than that, maybe no school tomorrow!

I bounded out of bed, walked over to the window, and realized it must have been snowing for some time without my noticing. Everything dazzled in white. The mailbox took on a different shape. A few tire tracks zig-zagged side by side on the street. I opened the sash with surprising ease—it was usually jammed shut due to the swelling of summer humidity—and stuck my head out, letting the giant snowflakes land softly on my hair. Quietness blanketed the landscape along with brilliant white, and I thought I could hear every snowflake landing on the evergreen tree outside my window. I knew I was in the middle of something special.

That night was an exclamation mark on my belief. My soul had no doubts in that moment that God was real. And I have been more convinced every year since.

Deep inside of us, in the place we often refer to as the soul, lies a custom made space designed to cradle belief. Crafted with the proper height, width and depth, this space is able to touch everything we experience. Those experiences are catalysts for something essential to human existence: belief.

Belief is a two-sided coin. On one side, belief is a choice, a volitional activity. Choosing to believe, like all choices, extends from the mind or the heart and is based, once again, on sensory data. I believe because I see, hear, taste, touch, smell. I believe that playoffs are a real possibility because I see the lineup and hear the sports analysts. I believe the claim that the creamery in the neighboring town makes the world's best ice cream because I smelled the waffle cones upon walking in, and saw the blackberries protruding from the purple swirls on a double dipped cone, and finally *tasted* it for myself. I believe the pool will be warm enough for a night swim because it's early August, and a perfectly executed cannonball inadvertently splashed me with refreshing water as I walked toward the diving board. In short, available data helps us believe.

But there's more to it than that. Much like our five senses, feelings also move us toward belief. Actually, what we feel can be even more convincing than what we see or hear. Our deepest feelings will be, whether we like it or not, more likely to foster belief than a hundred pages of survey results. Sure, that can get us into trouble once in a while when we lose our minds to the flare-up of emotions. We humans have a propensity to leave common sense at the door when our passions find high ground. An angry and resentful mob blames a store owner for the arrest of one of their cousins, so they break the large, plate glass windows with a cinder block. But the truth is, the store owner never once laid eyes on the alleged criminal. The vandalism was based entirely on emotion. Facts took second place to feelings. Nothing inspires misplaced hatred more than whispers down the lane, causing us to think with our emotions rather than with our minds.

The power of emotions isn't always a bad thing, however. Our feelings and our senses both influence us toward belief, and there are times when the two work in conjunction. Our five senses, coupled with feelings, create an intertwining ability to sustain the weight of belief, like a steel cable supporting the gondola a thousand feet above the valley. But when data enters the mix? When facts agree with emotions and our senses? You have a permanent change, the strongest of all beliefs.

When salt is added to water, it doesn't just add flavor. The entire molecular structure actually changes. Sodium chloride dissociates into sodium and chlorine ions. Water molecules are then attracted to the ions and vise-versa. Taste and scientific observation leave no doubt that something unique has happened. Belief is much like that. What we sense mixes with what we feel, like the water mixes with salt. And the end result is something useful—for brining, and even for healing.

So on one side of the coin, we choose what to believe, whether through deeper thinking, deeper feeling, sensory data, or better yet, all three. Let's call this side of the coin, *heads*.

Tails is something different altogether. The other side of the coin has a serendipitous shimmer to it. Rather than choosing belief, belief pounces on us.

Several summers ago, I walked around a zoo with my wife, three kids, and dripping ice cream cones. We stopped every twenty steps to see what furry critter lived in the next cage, in hopes they wouldn't be hiding in a box or behind a tree. The cages, made from a metal frame with chain-link fencing and painted forest green, seemed to grow in size as we moved along the hot asphalt path. I noticed one cage full of trees, propped up limbs, and rock cliffs, and a sign hanging on the padlocked gate that read "mountain lion." We stood for ten minutes trying to spot the large cat. Nothing. Until I turned to my left. The mountain lion had sneaked up behind us (don't worry, the steel bars and chain-link fence guaranteed our safety). I was shocked that we were completely unaware of its approach. As we watched the stealthy movement of the big cat and the efficiency of their silent-but-deadly padded paws, I began to understand what pouncing *really* meant. Mountain lions, as all cats do, patiently and softly approach their prey. They crouch, bound, then attack. A struggle ensues—often short-lived—and the cat gets the mouse, or rabbit, or antelope. The bigger the cat, the bigger the prey.

This side of belief is much like that. Quietly, things are happening in your life that are moving you in a direction of belief. You are unaware of these machinations until the moment of pouncing. A struggle ensues, and belief wins. In a sweeping, all-encompassing event, belief hooks its claws in us. We call that a God moment. We often say we "saw God" or "heard God." Or, better yet, we say something more formidable—we *found* God.

Humans are hardwired to believe. It's the way we were created. God sends a current, and we have the capacity to accept and conduct that current. We call that belief. So, God, who desires to be known, sends signals, pulses of electric currents which find their way to our minds and hearts. Sometimes it's *heads,* where I saw, felt or heard something and I believe. And sometimes it's *tails,* where in the midst of a cracked bulb and the silence of falling snow, belief lands on us in one fresh breeze and we just accept.

Belief is rooted in faith. As a matter of fact, in some languages the two words are synonymous.

A strong faith is based on a strong belief and a strong belief leads toward a strong faith. The key to understanding the relationship between faith and belief is the undergirding. A six-lane bridge will only hold the travelers and truck drivers if the steel underneath can support not only the weight, but the weather as well. Wind, rust and flooding have destroyed many a bridge. In the same way, belief has to be directed at something bigger than the word itself; "just believe" generates a question (in what?) and requires something bigger than us for an answer. Belief must be directed at something outside of ourselves if it is to be most powerful. The object of belief has to be bigger than self, something more substantial than wishful and positive thinking no matter how much gray matter we put into it. This belief has to withstand the rumble of heavy trucks, the battering of a hurricane, and the chronic malady of rust. In other words, that which we place our faith and belief in has to be more sturdy than ourselves.

That doesn't mean that having such belief is always easy. Belief and faith, by nature, involves a level of uncertainty. Some people agonize over their lingering sense of doubt which accompanies their uncertainty. But, it has to be that way. Think about it: if there was no doubt, there would be no such thing as faith or belief. Just like if there was no ugliness, there would be no such thing as beauty. Doubt will always attempt to cast its shadow on the path you walk, but faith is the assurance of something unseen, something hoped for in the near and far future. Therefore, the unseen things, including the future, must be evaluated based on something else besides our senses. We call that faith.

The certainty of our faith grows when belief is allowed the authority in us to move our feet, choose our words, use our hands, and develop thoughts in a way commensurate with that belief. Whether I choose to believe or I am taken by it, either way, it is part of me. Some say faith is a tool, one of the many in our toolbox used to navigate the life we have been given. Only this tool—and this tool alone—allows us to lay hold of the things of God.

Maybe the sun pressed its subtle heat upon his eyelids until they opened, the light triggering a splitting headache. Maybe he tossed all night long on his burlap, too much on his mind. Whatever it was, something was under Jesus's skin that day.

He woke to the breaking of sticks and the smell of fresh fire. One of the disciples had cooked breakfast, giving Jesus the opportunity to start the day slowly. But Jesus did not partake in breakfast. Maybe he was fasting. Maybe there was no time for him to eat. A busy day loomed ahead—crowds to teach, heal, and love; religious leaders to rebuke, challenge and instruct. That morning, "...as they were leaving Bethany, Jesus was hungry. He noticed a fig tree in full leaf a little way off, so he went over to see if he could find any figs. But there were only leaves, because it was too early in the season for fruit. Then Jesus said to the tree, "May no one ever eat your fruit again!" And the disciples heard him say it" (Mark 11:12-14).

Why did this happen? To be honest, Jesus may have been just plain tired, and a tad "hangry." Some days are just harder than others.

Jesus, as was his custom, walked to the temple with a desire to offer his prayers. But upon arriving, something didn't look right. The outer court looked like a flea market. The hustle of the crowds, loud voices, and the sound of money thrown onto the tables of money changers set the scene. Jesus believed deeply that the temple was, first and foremost, a house of prayer, not a mall for shopping. With a little investigation, Jesus discovered the core of the activity. It was a holiday season, and during this holiday, people were obliged to buy animals for various sacrificial rituals. Taking advantage of the holidays, the religious leaders set up shop and charged far too much for sheep, cattle, turtle doves, and pigeons. Obligation and guilt emptied the purses of the rich and poor alike, and the religious leaders unlawfully profited.

Immediately after realizing this, Jesus's pulse raced. Anger flooded him and reddened his cheeks– he grabbed the nearest table and hurled it across the floor of the outer courtyard. The crowds yelled with shaking fists. Ignoring them, he yanked another table—coins flew, bouncing and rolling with the shrill akin to the sound of broken glass.

"Get these things out of here! Stop turning my Father's house into a marketplace!" Jesus cried (John 2:16). "My Temple will be called a house of prayer for all nations, but you have turned it into a den of thieves" (Mark 11:17).

This infuriated the religious leaders, so much so that they made plans to kill him. So Jesus left, and his disciples—reluctant at first due to the outburst rarely seen in their Master—followed.

Belief stirs the deepest of passions, and that can be exhausting. The next day, Jesus rested with his disciples around the morning campfire before walking the dusty road back toward Jerusalem. Peter, in a moment of incredulity, walked by the now dead tree which Jesus had cursed the day before, reminding everyone that a miracle happened.

"Look, Rabbi! The fig tree you cursed has withered and died!" (Mark 11:20).

Jesus, in a teachable moment, offered profound hope and power in light of that miracle, and in light of belief.

"Have faith in God. I tell you the truth, you can say to this mountain, 'May you be lifted up and thrown into the sea,' and it will happen. But you must really believe it will happen and have no doubt in your heart" (Mark 11:23).

A bold promise. In that statement, he wove a common thread between belief and God, one that will become a beautiful tapestry if embroidered to the last stitch. Jesus made it clear that belief in God affects our everyday life. Every situation we encounter—a "hello" to a neighbor on the way to work, a conversation with your aged mother about geraniums, a decision you make at work, the birth of your daughter—everything is a stitch. Even a fig tree along the road not quite bearing fruit, and overturned tables in the courtyard of the temple are meant to stitch common threads of belief. God is weaving something, so your belief in God as the tailor means you trust him to make sense of it and use it for your good. You, faith, life, and God—if woven together, like an Amish quilt, these elements will tell a story of belief, self, and God's intersection with the here-and-now. You may only see the underside, a fuzzy image of the true picture, but God sees the finished product, the top side of the tapestry. Just believe God for this moment and the next. Fairly simple, really.

Once, a Roman soldier approached Jesus with a request to heal his paralyzed servant. The centurion came with nothing more than faith and belief. He believed Jesus could bring healing if only he might be willing. Not only was Jesus willing, but he even offered to walk the distance to visit with the afflicted servant.

This military leader would not have that. The soldier told Jesus there was no need for him to walk at all. He was so powerful that he could merely say the word—as the soldier does so many times a day with his subordinates—and the healing would be done.

Jesus's response? "I tell you the truth, I haven't seen faith like this in all Israel" (Matt. 8:10).

Jesus said the word, and it was done. Later, when the man discovered what time the servant became well again, he knew it was the same moment Jesus had spoken words of healing, miles away. Belief welled up within him. His sheer desperation and courage to ask allowed Jesus to pour his grace down upon him and his servant. Belief yields those types of results.

This hardwiring to believe predisposes us to another instinctual compulsion: that of worship. In other words, everyone worships something. We have no choice as to *whether* we will worship. We only have the choice in what or whom we worship. Some people worship possessions, some worship their jobs or their skills, some worship God, some worship singers, actors, or athletes. Some call it obsession—which, if you think about, can be quite alarming. We could end up believing in and even worshiping something that is unworthy of worship, or that simply has no capability to hold our life up.

Who or what holds your life together? Who or what is the "ultimate" for you? Is that "something" worthy to be worshiped? Can it be trusted to never let you down? In a moment of honesty, press down on those questions and take them to their end. Our hardwiring creates in us a void which will only be filled by belief. Belief raises a flag that signals to us its necessity and power. It tells us that our wholeness is at stake. But belief also raises another flag, one that points us to believe in something substantial, real, and not imagined or wished. These are ideas worth thinking about.

Jesus perceived the gravity of asking and answering these questions. Knowing that humans are hardwired to worship *something*, whether that something proves empty or fulfilling, Jesus focused his teaching on knowing the difference. The people were ready. They sat, stood, and leaned on olive trees—men and women and children perched all around, filling any space they could to see and hear the Master. He taught unforgettable lessons with an unmatched authority. In the middle of one particular teaching, Jesus juxtaposed two entities which, without doubt, will battle for their souls.

"No one can serve two masters. For you will hate one and love the other; you will be devoted to one and despise the other. You cannot serve God and be enslaved to money" (Matt. 6:24).

Hard truth.

Is there anything on this earth more tempting to worship than money? Money and possessions have barbs which attach quickly and prove painful to remove. There is nothing like material possessions to send us off the tracks when God is trying to keep us on a direct path toward him. Jesus's statement has much to say between the lines. Essentially, he asks the crowd to set God on one side of the page, money on the other, and ask these questions: Who or what holds your life together? Is that "something" worthy to be worshiped? Can it be trusted to never let you down? These same questions are directed at us. The sad truth is, we can't worship both God and money. For Jesus to focus on the two candidates of potential worship, it only stands to reason that this could be the most important crossroad at which we will ever arrive. Be sure to stop, ponder, and read the signs. Then turn. Choose wisely which of the two is ultimately worthy of belief, faith, and worship.

So, there we have it. Two sides of the same coin. On the one side, senses—upon hearing the teaching, seeing the cursed fig tree, or feeling his hand on a shoulder, they made a logical choice to follow Jesus. On the other, serendipity—Jesus showed up and just like people who accidentally smack their heads into a fencepost because they were too busy watching their feet, they were jolted into belief. Either way, something inside knows when belief has arrived. It changes us, because it fills the space created for it.

In our modern times, with the accelerated pace of technological advancement and the complexity of science and biomedicine, the incongruity of two seemingly opposing forces (belief in God and knowledge which we gain through our senses and study) lands harder upon us now than in antiquity. Those who declare that a belief in God is said to work rather well with our empirical senses, biological research, and astronomy, are in the minority. But no matter how brilliant we become, or how far we advance, it is difficult to ignore the hardwiring within.

What do I do with this idea of belief, this space inside me longing to be filled? I let it do what it is meant to do—I allow it to point me to God. To believe in God is to invite him into my life, my mess, my goals, my dreams, my disappointments. It is to see God as relevant and powerful and near. It is to accept his love and grace and a reaching hand that is bent on rescuing, a hand that tends to me.

Once, when the disciples asked Jesus what they might do to follow him more fervently and serve God more diligently, he answered simply, "This is the only work God wants from you: believe in the one he has sent" (John 6:29). Go with it, and you will find out for yourself. Take belief to its very end and let *heads* fill your mind and heart, and *tails* fill your soul.

WONDER

"He to whom the emotion is a stranger, who can no longer pause to wonder and stand wrapped in awe, is as good as dead— his eyes are closed."

Albert Einstein

"The world is full of magic things, patiently waiting for our senses to grow sharper."

W.B. Yeats

My wife and I boarded a trans-Atlantic flight to Eastern Europe early in March, 2023. We were visiting our daughter, who was spending a year in Bosnia, engaged in nonprofit work to serve the people there by teaching English and helping lead a community center. The plane touched down just after lunch in Sarajevo, a major city in what was formerly known as Yugoslavia. Currently the capital city of Bosnia, Sarajevo boasts a vast, idyllic, snow-capped mountain range that surrounds the entire city on all sides. The city stretches longways like a bowling alley while two parallel roads connect all parts of the city end to end.

The mountains captured my attention and while driving through the city, a thought clicked: I could take my daughter snowboarding on the same mountain which was the site of the 1984 Winter Olympics. The potential for a great day on the slopes echoed from the mountains. A high five sealed the deal.

We drove an old Toyota RAV up the windy steeps, passed the colorful Olympic rings in the center of a turnabout, and parked in the stone lot. In my twenty-five-plus years of snowboarding, I never once snowboarded outside the east coast of the United States, which made the anticipation of this day of riding *epic*. I imagined the former winter athletes riding the bus multiple times on this same road and it stirred me, as it always does when tracing the footsteps of great people in history. You feel what they felt and, through that, we somehow connect to all of humanity.

The weather proved almost perfect, and the boarding was phenomenal. Blue skies created a canopy against the white mountains. Sunshine lit the slopes and reflected off the snow into our squinted eyes. The snow on the sidewalks looked like spilled coconut slushies. Every half hour, snow flurries dropped in to remind us it was still winter. As the day came to a close, we decided to gear up and ride the chairlift to the peak one more time. Halfway to the top, however, we slid into the dense fog of a low-hanging cloud. Being unfamiliar with the mountain and its trails, we knew that riding with this lack of visibility would prove challenging. The three-seat chairlift slowly ascended to the top, breaking through the other side of that cloud. The fog opened up into blue skies like a can of paint poured over a gray canvas.

We strapped in our boots and started descending. Rounding a downhill corner, we immediately stopped. The last of the clouds floated by like a velvet stage curtain, revealing the grandest, largest, most beautiful, pointed, wrinkled, crisp, and clear mountains either of us have ever seen. Blue skies, gray rock, with white in every crevice and poured over the top like marshmallow cream. We sat down together in the snow. It was all we could do. Nothing we had seen before even came close to this beauty.

I whispered, "Wow!" and she declared, "Thank you, God!"

These were the only two appropriate responses in the face of such magnificence.

True wonder never immediately evokes verbosity; rather, it ignites an explosion of only one or two words. Wonder takes us to a different place, to new heights, to vast openness, and to an awareness that intrigue and beauty are an irresistible combination. The truth is, our days are filled with this kind of wonder. Wonder is all around us, waiting for us to notice those things—big and small, simple and complex—which waken it, rousing in us a sense of something far more, far bigger than our minds alone can take us. We just have a hard time slowing down to a pace where the search for wonderful things are on our radar. We rush from thing to thing, erasing the margin our lives needed to catch a glimpse of wonder when it sneaks up on us. We have a hard time removing ourselves, even just momentarily, from the stress we carry which ultimately acts as blinders, shading the eminence of wonder. We have a hard time peeling away from electronic devices enough to see the puff of a dandelion floating its seeds to faraway places. But we must. Wonder is a catalyst to happiness and contentment. And, so, it is very good for us to find wonder in everyday life.

Who hasn't seen a sunset over the water that almost makes you cry? Who hasn't touched the soft fur of goslings, and puppies, and kittens, and baby goats? Who hasn't seen a surprise snowfall cover the piles of trash and old cars, converting all of it into photo-worthy material? Who hasn't looked up at a midnight sky, clear as a bell, and perceived layer upon layer of stars? I sat on a curb at a convenience store with my wife to eat lunch and picked a flower no bigger than the eraser on a number two pencil, yet containing all the petals and pistils of any flower ten times its size. Brilliant. I received a text recently from someone who saw a female oriole in her front yard and asked God, if he cared, to send a male. Within minutes, an orange-breasted male landed on her feeder. And it changed her. There is a reason things are called wonder-*ful*.

Much of wonder stems from nature, and for good reason. The ancient scripture passage says, "The heavens declare the glory of God, the skies proclaim the work of his hands" (Psalm 19:1). "Lift up your eyes on high and see who has created these stars. The One who leads forth their host by number, He calls them all by name; Because of the greatness of His might and the strength of His power, not one of them is missing" (Isaiah 40:26).

I am overcome when I look far into the blackest nights, but I can also stand dumbfounded when I see what humans have accomplished. A bridge that spans miles over the bay, footers running deep into bedrock under fathoms of water. Airplanes and ships, mammoth machines that shake their fists at gravity and buoyancy, so heavy but still able to fly or float. A skyscraper that moves like a tall oak tree in the wind but doesn't fall over. A dam wall that restrains millions upon millions of gallons of water. I often find myself awestruck by the ingenuity of fellow humans. I thought I understood the breadth of human-made wonder until I saw Venice, and stood on the bridge with my mouth wide open, unable to say a word.

Architecture surely inspires wonder, but much of the wonder I experience when looking into the extraordinary things produced by people has to do with art. The entire field of the arts are a progeny of wonder. Music, painting, sculpture, photography, writing, poetry, pottery, songwriting—on and on the list goes, and they all begin at a moment of inspiration, and they all go on to cause wonder. Inspiration itself is bathed in wonder.

Art moves me, and at times stuns me. How can someone capture the emotions of sitting at a cafe with enough detail to feel the connection, but enough obscurity to make me fill in the blanks? How does that framed black-and-white photograph pass through my eyes directly to my heart? That is the power of art.

I walked through a furniture consignment store recently while the speakers in the ceiling played a rather good playlist. One of my all-time favorite songs piped through and landed right in my soul. I smiled and involuntarily said, "Yes!" I found an old chair, pulled it directly under a ceiling speaker which looked more like a shower head, and let the music flow. I leaned my head on a tag cut from an old manilla folder and was transported to another place for six whole minutes. How did that artist put together the lyrics, the chords, the groove in such a way that it all felt right, that the universe is in order? I sat in wonder.

A dancer performs a series of spins then floats to the other side of the stage, gliding ghost-like, gracefully. How does she do that? A street vendor constructs a toy airplane from a used tin can. What? A man with three different sized chainsaws takes a tree stump and turns it into a bear eating a fish. Are you kidding me? All I can do is watch and wonder.

Some say the primary thing that sets us apart from animals is art. We are inspired when we see a perfectly spun spiderweb, so we paint it, photograph it, write a poem of its symmetry and its delicate strength. The spider merely wants to catch bugs, but we experience wonder and awe at the sight of her methods to do so. It changes us in a way that we are compelled to capture that, somehow. Capturing the moment, the essence, the memory brings to us meaning accrued over a lifetime.

Wonder drives the tent peg of art to a deeper place inside of us, giving us a canopy, a space in which we can isolate ourselves from the hurry of our lives and breathe in the moment. The point is, we are fortunate to have the capacity to sense wonder at all.

Wonder exhales what amazement inhales. There are just too many things beyond comprehension, or indescribably beautiful, or miraculous to not live with a sense of wonder and awe. This fact, once again, points us to something far beyond ourselves, something beyond the reality of our five senses. It points us to the grandeur of the eternal artist who created this intoxicating fresco called Earth. Artists have been painting images of it ever since we learned to make paint. Birds, sunsets, flowers, oceans, portraits, farmland, storm clouds, have covered many a canvas—made of cotton paper, stucco, or cave walls—for millennia. Wonder is the catalyst for all of it. Art attempts to display, define, and interpret wonder.

Wonder has a goal: to awaken in us a sense of supernatural involvement. In the ancient world, the appearance of supernatural activity and involvement were called signs and wonders. An awe-evoking event (sign) activated a sense of mystery and amazement (wonder). The senses grabbed hold (sign), and the senses beheld (wonder). It was said of Jesus by the people who knew him best, "God publicly endorsed Jesus the Nazarene by doing powerful miracles, wonders, and signs through him, as you well know" (Acts 2:22). And they well knew. Wonder kindled a flame in all who heard and saw Jesus. The mystery and power and wisdom of Jesus turned people's attention to the phenomenon of God's nearness. Ancient writings pointed to the reality of God causing "wonders in the heavens above and signs on the earth below..." (Joel 2:30).

On a memorable night, the occasional bleating of sheep filled the calmness of the air—air that was also infused with signs and wonders. Shepherds walked slowly in their worn leather sandals, crooked staff in hand. While nothing was particularly different about that night, something deep inside them said there would be.

Suddenly, above! Angels! "Don't be afraid!" one of them said. "I bring you good news that will bring great joy to all people. The Savior—yes, the Messiah, the Lord—has been born today in Bethlehem" (Luke 2:10-11).

Then the angels sang. The shepherds began their swift journey to Bethlehem and before long, they gazed upon a woman who gave birth to a child called Jesus, the one who warranted an angelic escort upon his arrival.

Some time later, a group of "magi," wise counselors and astrologers from the east, saw something in the night skies which sent them packing their camels in preparation for a long journey across the desert to the Holy Land. Being unsure of the exact location, they waited, studied the maps, followed the celestial stars and planets, and sat to discuss how they might find the one whom the stars announced.

Suddenly, above! A star never seen before! It hung low enough to point them to the newborn King. "And the star they had seen in the east guided them to Bethlehem. It went ahead of them and stopped over the place where the child was. When they saw the star, they were filled with joy! They entered the house and saw the child with his mother, Mary, and they bowed down and worshiped him. Then they opened their treasure chests and gave him gifts of gold, frankincense, and myrrh" (Matt. 2:9-11). A song by an angel choir, a virgin woman giving birth, wise men led by a star. The wonder of it all.

It seemed the beginning of Jesus's life on earth foretold the many signs and wonders which would accompany him years later. Jesus became this intriguing figure, of whom his undeniable power pointed to one thing—God. Crowds followed him. They saw the miraculous signs. They heard his teaching. They sensed in his presence the supernatural. They drew nearer to God just being by his side or catching a glimpse of him walking the streets.

Two such "sign and wonder" episodes in the life of Jesus caught my attention recently. The first is when Jesus turned water into wine. Let that sink in for a minute. Water, the simple compound H_2O, turned into a completely different chemical and physical compound, bearing relatively little resemblance to water.

The other morning, I ran out of milk after having poured Frosted Flakes into a stainless mixing bowl (I was too hungry to clean a cereal bowl) to enjoy my breakfast. All morning long I anticipated, with much excitement, the crunch and taste of sugar and the instant rush that would go through my body after five spoonfuls. But wait, no milk? What now? My morning was ruined. After holding my face in my hands for a few seconds, an idea popped into my head: I could use water.

Then I thought the very same thing you just thought, and tossed the idea aside, pouring all the cereal back into the box.

But what if I did fill the bowl with water, and then when I said some kind of thanks or blessing over it, it turned to milk?

Impossible. I would have freaked out...but I'm fairly sure it would have been delicious, if I didn't decide first to toss it over the railing of my back porch from the abhorrence of water turning milky white. The point is, to turn water into wine requires a bonafide miracle.

The wooden frame was just large enough to hang dried flowers and fruits along the lattice work on the gray, faded trellis, giving it an earth-tone beauty for the bride and groom. The courtyard was full, and the wedding reception had begun. Merriment and laughter bounced off the stone walls. The sound of woodwind instruments, tambourines, and hand drums filled every empty space.

Then, one relatively major concern arose: the wine jars emptied before they should have. It turns out that the large crowd at this particular wedding drank too much (some things never change). Families who hosted weddings always tried to avoid running out of wine for fear of dishonoring the guests or disgracing their family name, or both. But there was nothing to do. What's gone is gone.

Jesus's mother, however, gave attention to the matter. She was, after all, an invited guest and everyone wants to see a wedding go well, especially moms. Mary immediately thought of a clever solution. Her son, miraculous from the day he was born, could do something. But what? And would he? She brought it to his attention, then left the problem in Jesus's hands.

After hearing from his mother that wine had gone dry, Jesus and a few servants quietly entered a room where six 30-gallon, stone, ceremonial jars stored water used for religious purposes. The door was closed. Quietness surrounded them. Whatever he did in the next few minutes—whether a prayer, or a touch—the water suddenly darkened, then transformed into a brilliant, crimson wine.

Astounding! Immediately, a cup was given to the master of the ceremony. He sniffed, then tasted, then looked around. He silenced the crowd, announcing to everyone that the best wine has been saved until now. Problem solved. The new wine filled the jars. The wonder of it all filled their hearts. "This sign at Cana was the first time Jesus revealed his glory. And his disciples believed him" (John 2:11).

Jesus evoked awe in that moment. To those who knew what he did, "how" was the primary interrogative. But I am struck by the "why." Running out of wine was not a life-or-death situation. No one's physical health needed attention. No one needed healing from leprosy, blindness, or malformation. Nor did anyone need food. The sign and wonder performed at the wedding stemmed from pure grace. The precedent set at that miracle, one of many yet to come, showed something quite remarkable: that this all-powerful, ever-present God cares about even the smallest details of our lives—an incomprehensible wonder, indeed.

The many miracles which followed bore witness to the wonder that surrounded Jesus. The sick were healed. The hungry were fed. The miserable were set free. The blind received sight. Even the dead were raised. While the wonder of nature points us towards this transcendent, magnificent God, who lives beyond our comprehension, the person of Jesus stokes an ember in us of God's nearness.

I am always aware of the healing power and love of God after I get sick. Fever, headaches, nausea, and muscle aches require rest and attention. I always pray during this time. I am doubly aware and sensitive to what others feel when they are going through the same thing, especially my kids. So I pray for them, too. And thanks to God, a few days later they are better. These minor sicknesses, while annoying and potentially dangerous, usually are not. But I have much compassion for those with chronic illness.

In the second story which caught my attention, Jesus healed an outcast: a forgotten, marginalized, contagious leper.

After having preached to the crowds, Jesus descended the grassy hillside. Large crowds, once again, followed. Jesus and those standing next to him heard a bit of commotion behind them. They turned to see the cause of the murmuring. Out of nowhere, a leper stammered toward Jesus. Another version of this account, written by a doctor, states that this was an advanced case of leprosy. His torn clothes stained with years of dirt, his sweaty skin, and his deformed hand meant one thing: stay away, or this will happen to you, too. The crowd scattered, covering their faces for fear of contracting the deadly disease.

Jesus, however, remained still. There was no panic in Jesus's face, only compassion as he smiled, eyes welling up as the leper approached and knelt before him.

"Lord," the man said. "If you are willing, make me clean" (Matt. 8:2).

The next words draw us into wonder: "Jesus reached out and touched him" (Matt. 8:3). It is advised to never touch a leper, and as a matter of fact, the very act of touching a leper was against religious law at that time. If there was one thing to never do at the approach of a leper, Jesus did the very opposite. He actually and willfully *touched* the leper.

I do not believe that he had to. Other miracles Jesus performed were done at the sound of his words. The profundity here is in the proximity. The contact was calculated. In that gesture, Jesus desired to communicate something radical and unforeseen. He demonstrated nearness, near enough to touch, tender enough to care, powerful enough to heal. That is the wonder.

Jesus responded to the leper's request: "I am willing" (Matt. 8:3). The rest is history.

God sends signs. Some you see, some you hear, and some you feel. What signs have plucked the strings of wonder in your heart lately? What causes the wonder that reverberates deep inside you? A mountaintop? A song? A bee? A friend? A picnic among the chatter of birds and laughter of children? Was it recovery? Or the right word at the right time?

The world is full of wonder. So often, though, we miss the opportunity to wonder. We hurry by the seemingly insignificant things, passing them off as commonplace. Someone once told me that God gets our attention in the big things, but shows off in the little things. I like that. Either way, God is interested in pointing your heart and mind toward him. This makes God *wonder*ful, this God who does *wonder*ful things, who captures us in moments of *wonder*ment. We merely need to slow down enough to allow it in.

PURPOSE

"The mystery of human existence lies not in just staying alive, but in finding something to live for."

Fyodor Dostoyevsky

"Purpose is the place where your deep gladness meets the world's needs."

Frederick Buechner

My daughter and I stepped off the inbound train at Jefferson Station. It was the day of our annual trip to the Philadelphia Flower Show, something we have enjoyed together since she was six years old. The anticipation of seeing the spectacular flower arrangements from floor to ceiling, smelling the floral-scented air, and hearing the chatter of the crowds amid the euphonic string quartet was palpable. But first—lunch.

The Convention Center was mostly built on the structures of the historic Reading Railroad Terminal, a massive indoor shed where trains would pull in, park, and pick up and drop off passengers.

The ground floor of this immense building hosts the famous Reading Terminal Market, an indoor public market that began in 1893 and still operates in much the same way today. Over one hundred merchants offer freshly prepared meals or meats to take home for later. Fresh vegetables, fish over ice, artisan cheeses, coffee beans, ice cream, and candy fill the glass counters and shelves. A few jewelers, woodworkers, and clothiers sell merchandise from around the world. But we came for lunch.

With so many options, so many flavors, so many lines of people, how will we ever choose? We choose by walking. Following our nose. We feel it. It's the only way. With so many specialty and ethnic foods—Asian or Cajan? Deli or fried? Mexican or Island? Philly cheesesteak or Maryland crab cake?—it's no small feat. And then you have to choose dessert—cannoli from the Italian bakery? Or whoopie pies from the Amish? The vendors take pride in their craft. A rewarding day for them consists of two things: making money and seeing a smile on the faces of those who can't wait to open the styrofoam lid and dive in.

And then there are the vendors who are chosen to represent their company within the actual flower show itself. They agree to the yearly theme—whether Legends of Ireland, or Islands of Aloha, or

Wonders of Water, or Flower Power—and create flower beds, yards, and even small buildings. These vendors are mostly high-end landscapers and hardscapers who have the means to host a flower-and-landscape display in the largest indoor flower show in the world.

For those who create these ornate displays, flowers are what they do; floral is what gets them up in the morning. We all have our thing, our predisposition, our leaning, or our bent. For many, it's not as visible as a 2000-foot display of greenery and colorful blossoms, or a bustling marketplace stall. But for everyone, their "bent" is just as significant to the meaning of their existence. That predilection is something that both makes us tick and makes the world a better place.

As we walked across the busy street toward the flower show, I noticed a young man in his mid-20s, who was fairly well dressed, holding the door to a public building connecting the market to the convention center. The entrance and exit accommodated a constant flow of people. He worked neither for the flower show nor the market. Not even the city. *He will want a tip,* I thought, and I would oblige if the opportunity arose, merely because he did a good thing, with everyone holding flowers and lunch and oranges and candy for the way home.

It was our turn. We walked to the door; he opened it, and wished both of us a blessed day. I pulled a few loose dollars from my front pocket, but to my surprise, he refused. I insisted he get some coffee on this cold day. Again, no. In a few words, he explained that he just wanted to make people's day better.

We all have our thing.

There is a vast difference between what you are good at, how much you accomplish, and your purpose. Of course, when those three conjoin, the result is a beautiful trifecta. Our skillset is likely related to our purpose once that deeper, authentic, existential purpose is discovered (which is not as hard to determine as one may think). How much we accomplish can also be related to our purpose, but not necessarily so. I know quite a few people, and hear of many more, for whom the acquisition of wealth and the increase of fame has left them notably unhappy. For those lamentable souls, the mantra is the same: there has to be more.

The accumulation of years tends to bring a perspective that activates a "rethink" switch. The rethink switch asks questions directly related to purpose. I'm not talking about familiar and frequent questions of the tame sort, like, who might I have lunch with today? What shirt would look good with jeans? What color shall I paint the wall? Do I feel like running on the treadmill? These questions are like lightswitches—common and easy to flip.

In moments of deeper contemplation, however, it's not merely a lightswitch—it's a lever. Lever switches halt and release enormous energy, power, or information. Lever switches we use seldomly, or not at all, so they are not frequent, and not familiar. A lever "rethink" switch asks life-altering questions. What contributions have I made? Why do I feel the way I do? What is truly important? What is life all about? Am I happy? What legacy can I leave? Do I have purpose here? What will make my life count?

I believe that every human being who has ever existed on this planet, and whoever will, have at least these three things in common: we are created in the image of God; we have a legitimate place on this earth; we desire to contribute something meaningful. Those three principles, burrowed out of deeper questions, have everything to do with purpose because it has to do with something else humans need: significance. Significance, defined in those three ways, sprouts deep roots. If we do not believe that we in some ways resemble God, that we are here for a reason, and that we desire to contribute something meaningful in this world, then we are left to rummage through life like searching in an abandoned storage unit, looking for a thing of value but never really finding it. Enough tries like that and you eventually quit.

Everybody has value, and not in varying degrees. We are so accustomed to see things through the lens of increased and potential value that we forget that there is such a thing as intrinsic value.

I remember going to a jeweler in downtown Baltimore to to pick a diamond for an engagement ring. They called him King. Nice man. I asked no questions. He opened the safe, pulled a manilla envelope, and out poured diamonds, scattering onto the papers which were strewn over his desk. With an eyepiece on, he told me the value of each diamond and why. Depending on the cut, color, clarity and carat, (the four Cs) the price would rise or fall. Some were extremely valuable, some not. I must have chosen a good one because she said yes. And because I became instantly broke.

The same principle applies when looking for a home to buy. Location, school district, square footage, acreage, and quality of the house all work to drive the price up or down. Similarly, we can determine the price of antiques lying around the basement by figuring out its age and rarity—it just might be a rusted relic worth tens of thousands. Barn finds fascinate most people because we are aware of the concept of value.

Various factors are used to rate gems, antiques, tools, and collectables to determine a price. Not so with people. People have intrinsic value. There has never been or never will be a man or woman who was or is more valuable than another. Nor has there ever been or ever will be a man or woman who was or is less valuable than another. That is what intrinsic value means. And that kind of value has to come from somewhere else besides us, because some people—either through ignorance or insensitivity, or both—place differing degrees of value on people. That's just wrong, but it has happened for years. Race, religion, age, social status, gender, skill, wealth, vocation—like the four Cs of diamonds, traits like these tempt us to place a higher or lower value on human life. So sad. And then the ugly side of human nature creeps up, and the saying which probably first came from a seven-year-old on a playground, "I'm better than you," still slithers into our minds all these years later. Then we believe it. Then we say it.

But no. Every life has the same value, the same significance. That truth becomes the backdrop for the part you will play on the stage of this earth. You matter.

This takes us once again to something far beyond us. To ask if there is more to this life is to ask a simple yet weighty metaphysical question. In other words, if the life we live and sense with our five senses is all there is, then, ultimately, we are in danger of becoming a people whose primary interest is *self*. Hedonism, a philosophy of life in which the pursuit of pleasure and the avoidance of pain dominates all other passions, pursuits, and ambitions, sets ourselves as the center of the universe. We call it self-interest, self-preservation, or self-promotion. Something tragic happens under this philosophy: a profound sadness, at times inconsolable, develops. I had a nightmare once where a tombstone read, "Here he lies, having spent his whole life on himself." There has to be more.

If all people are created in the image of God, have a legitimate place on this earth, and desire to contribute something meaningful, then there *is* more. Far more. Something deep inside of all people yearns to make a difference, and when that opportunity arises—and you help fix a flat tire, buy a stranger a cup of coffee, encourage a friend with a few words, visit the old folks' home, give someone a second chance, compliment your wife, invite the new neighbor for a cookout—then a sense of

PURPOSE

usefulness, or helpfulness, bubbles to the surface. And that feels right. Gratifying. Like hearing the snap of a puzzle piece placed correctly.

My wife and I walked the sidewalks and back streets of an idyllic town along the Chesapeake Bay, conscious of the 19th century architecture up against the sun which raced downward, only a few hours from touching the water. The scenic river meets a historic wharf at the old hardware store, what is now an upscale restaurant. A car driven by an elderly woman, husband by her side, pulled alongside us and asked a question which I haven't been asked in quite a long time.

"Excuse me. Can you please tell me how to get to the restaurant at the wharf?"

That's all. I gave her directions and told both of them they would arrive within a few minutes and are sure to have a delicious meal. They deserved it, having been married for sixty years.

I paused after watching the two drive away. Wow, nice people. I couldn't help but feel the goodness of that interaction. A stranger asking a stranger for help. One party listening intently, one party sharing enthusiastically. Eye-to-eye contact. Smiles all around. A "thank you." An "enjoy the meal." GPS has all but taken that away from us. We live in such a high-tech, low face-to-face culture.

Primarily, though, I felt a sense of purpose. I used my expertise to help someone. I felt useful in that moment, and that stirred up warmth, vivacity. Funny how something so small can drum up something so joyful, so motivating. Taking the thought a step further, I actually helped someone accomplish a goal. That's a good way to do good in this world. We were created for that.

Think of a time when you explained to someone how to do a task—change a flat tire, learn a function on a smartphone, clip a dog's claws, bake the best chocolate chip cookies. I still remember my mom showing me how to separate the yolk from the white by transferring the glob inside the egg back and forth into the half shells. I made an entire mess the first time. I remember my dad showing me how to replace spark plugs on a motorcycle. I was ten years old. Thought I was big stuff. Handing skills to one another is essential to human thriving. When we do that, we help people thrive, and in so doing, fulfill a purpose for why we are here.

Eventually, the question arises: from where does this drive to help one another come?

PURPOSE

Jesus's legs wobbled a bit, having stumbled on a rock buried in the sand. His mouth parched, his foot starting to blister, he finally saw the thatched rooftops of the two-story buildings far in the distance. After walking miles through the arid wilderness, Jesus returned to his hometown. There, he began his public ministry. The signs and miracles which accompanied Jesus's teaching would soon demonstrate his divine nature, but in the beginning of his ministry, things were done a little more covertly. For instance, after he would heal people of their illnesses, he told those same people not to tell anyone what just happened (they usually ignored his request). It all seemed a little strange to his disciples. But Jesus said he would go public, soon. Soon, the world would have to look at this man and discern for themselves how to interpret his teaching, his power, his love. And it all started here in the penniless town of Nazareth.

On one particular day very early in Jesus's ministry, he visited the synagogue, as was customary for any devout Jew. There they could pray, worship God, and hear the Scriptures read while in the community of neighbors. It was asked of Jesus that day to read from the Prophets. Standing to read the Scriptures, all eyes were on this son of Mary and Joseph, who made their home in Nazareth, who taught their son the trade of carpentry in this very town. He held the scroll and paused longer than normal. Collecting his thoughts, he determined the time was right to state that which would characterize his life, preoccupy his mind, and determine his purpose. He had yet, as far as we know, to heal anyone, feed thousands, or turn water into wine. But his reading and subsequent commentary made it very clear he intended to. He slowly and deliberately unrolled the scroll, found the text he wanted to read, looked at the crowd, and began reciting the words.

"The scroll of Isaiah the prophet was handed to him. He unrolled the scroll and found the place where this was written:

'The Spirit of the Lord is upon me, for he has anointed me to bring Good News to the poor.

He has sent me to proclaim that captives will be released, that the blind will see, that the oppressed will be set free, and that the time of the Lord's favor has come.'

"He rolled up the scroll, handed it back to the attendant, and sat down. All eyes in the synagogue looked at him intently. Then he began to speak to them. "The Scripture you've just heard has been fulfilled this very day!" (Luke 4:17-21).

So beautiful, poetic, powerful, dramatic. I can feel the glare of the eyes, the astonished looks for hearing such claims. Tension in the room was palpable. I can imagine the conversations over flatbread and hummus later that day. Essentially, Jesus made some things unmistakably clear about himself. It's like he was saying, "I'm here now. Just like it was foretold. And my life is going to be about *others*. Not power, not politics, not jewels, not crowns. But people. Broken people with real needs. Bringing people to that 'Something More' is why I am here. Compassion, wholeness, healing, laughter, shoulder-to-shoulder love—that's how I do things." Staggering, when you think about it. One thing is for sure: Jesus had stated his grand purpose for his time on earth.

Everything about Jesus pointed to his passion for changing the lives of the people he loved. He desired to see them whole again, restored, reaffirmed. People, all people, hold immense value in the eyes and heart of Jesus.

To the crowds he said, "Look at the birds. They don't plant or harvest or store food in barns, for your Heavenly Father feeds them. And aren't you far more valuable to him than they are?" (Matt. 6:26). Value. A ton of it. And based on the fact that Jesus considers everyone to have intrinsic value, it only follows that every person also has built-in meaning and purpose.

Everyone. That includes you.

Jesus walked toward Jerusalem with his twelve disciples. A crowd followed who recently heard his teaching and witnessed his miracles. Jesus walked ahead of everyone else for no other reason than he needed time to think. And because the crowds didn't want to "disturb" the rabbi, they held back. The disciples, being in awe of the many things Jesus did and said, began conversing with one another.

Two of his disciples, James and John, in a moment of self-absorption, discussed how they'd like to sit on the throne with Jesus for all of eternity, one on his right and the other on his left. The by-product of this gift, if granted, was subsequently a position above everyone else. Upon overhearing some of the conversation, Jesus took an opportunity to challenge and correct their thinking. He immediately began explaining to the disciples a new way of living, a way Jesus himself modeled. In so doing, he restated another purpose for his life.

"But among you it will be different. Whoever wants to be a leader among you must be your servant, and whoever wants to be first among you must be the slave of everyone else. For even the Son of Man [a reference to himself] came not to be served, but to serve others and give his life as a ransom for many" (Mark 10:43-45).

That's a pretty good purpose statement.

To serve and not be served, to live for others, to put them first, to withhold my gain so someone else can thrive, to give my life to others—that's an elevated purpose. When our lives are lived for others, no matter our vocation—be it a chef, teacher, fireman, small business owner, landscaper, bank supervisor, etc.—*and* no matter our role in life—be it mom, dad, brother, sister, cousin, uncle, grandma, teammate, neighbor, classmate—we will come very close to discovering the intent of God for us, our grand purpose in life. Turns out, it's about others.

All of us are placed purposefully in this grand story of life. It's a story of doing the most good by serving the most people in our sphere of touch. Jesus did that. Serving, then, becomes a grand purpose. Purpose always comes from a higher place, a different plane, one that reaches far beyond self. Those higher places are the places which God informs and Jesus models. God gave you everything you need to add value to everyone and everything around you. Think of what you can lend your employee, your boss, your patient, your child, your friend.

That's how much God values you and all the contributions you make to serve, to make this world a better place. You are made for this. Purpose like that points to something far greater than you and me. It points to a God who cares equally for everyone, orchestrating a scenario where you take turns playing second fiddle, so the one next to you gets a moment to shine.

I go as far as to say that God put you here because someone needs you. You have a purpose, a meaningful contribution to make, and a legitimate place in making this world better, even if that means to hold the door for a thousand people a day.

EMPTINESS

"It was not the feeling of completeness I so needed, but the feeling of not being empty."

Jonathan Safron Foer

"There's just something obvious about emptiness, even when you try to convince yourself otherwise."

Sarah Dessen

I ran out of gas driving westbound on the Pennsylvania Turnpike, which could arguably be the worst place to do so. Even worse, it was my second time running out of gas on that same highway. I didn't think it was as entertaining as my friends seemed to, when I told them the story. They called me names. I get it. And probably deserved it. Running out of gas seems to be my thing. But I sort of fault the car. When the digital readout tells me I have a driving range of 30 more miles, I expect to be able to drive that distance. It at least affords me the time to find a gas station. I had no idea that thirty actually means fifteen.

So, I sat there on the shoulder with my family, waiting for one of those red-and-white rescue trucks with yellow flashing lights and the logo of a major insurance company plastered on the door to make sure everyone knows who the good neighbor actually is. I know from experience that they will give you five dollars worth of gas for free and send you on your way.

It's easy to tell when your car's gas tank is empty, or nearly so. Just look at the gauge. When the gauge nears empty, it's time to go fill the tank. Since we know how to fill it, no worries. But when things get really, really low, a new light on the dash which resembles a gas pump starts blinking. Often a tone dings at intervals to alert those completely unaware of their current situation. And when you really get to the very bottom of the tank, the engine stutters and you have only a few seconds to pull off to the side of the road. At least three options are available at that point: walk to a gas station with a can, call someone, or just wait for help. Not the ideal situation, but nor is it the worst. There are at least clear solutions to this problem.

I wish it were that easy with people.

I find similarities between cars and humans. Both expend energy. Both require refilling. Both possess indicators which help those who are attentive determine the approximate range they have in their current state. Both require attention when depleted. Stress, depression, anger, fatigue can be some of the indicators about which we speak. You won't get far overlooking any of those signs.

Our lives swarm with examples of the need for replenishment and refilling. A watering can, once full, sprinkles out its last drops on the marigolds. A cauldron of stew empties due to feeding two dozen hungry soldiers. A reservoir dries out while hydrating an entire city during a drought. The last four drops of pancake syrup crawl from the plastic figurine. People provide plentiful examples as well. We run and sweat and thirst for water. Calories are burned during a workout and we crave an energy bar. Brains are taxed to their limits after a study session and need more coffee. A hard conversation depletes our emotions and we crumble. We need filling because we spend energy.

All that makes sense. The emptiness about which I write, however, resides in another space altogether. You feel this kind of emptiness at a deeper place than the stomach, and it can sometimes go beyond what you see on a dashboard. As a matter of fact, it doesn't touch your five senses at all. This sort of emptiness can just come over you, a fast-moving cloud that dims your picnic blanket without warning. It doesn't shout—it patiently waits until the right moment, then darkly whispers.

We wake at three in the morning. Quietness, darkness, stillness. The whispering begins, subtly at first. Never loud, though palpable as the minutes tick by. Something stirs deep within, instigating perplexing questions we rattle through our minds like index cards. Not able to answer, or place what it is that bothers us, we try to fall back to sleep. 3:35 a.m. We wake to look at the red digits. 3:39 a.m. How can that be? Time slowed, bending the way Einstein said it does when in a black hole. We have no answers, but we have a rational explanation: something is missing.

Emptiness may be the best way to describe the feeling. And those sleepless, moonlit mornings prove to be the times we most hear its whispers. But the whisper of emptiness isn't required to show up only at night, when things are quiet, when our minds tend to race. It can also show up at other unexpected moments.

It was my senior year in high school. Our football and baseball team won the Maryland state championships that very same year, the only school in the history of Maryland high school sports to do so.

EMPTINESS

Five of us, including myself, played on both teams. I can still envision the playoff games leading up to the state championship game for each of those sports. And when we finally won, as you might expect, we as a team were elated—and so was Randallstown. (Go Rams!)

But I can also remember later that week feeling a bit deflated. We won. It's what we worked for, hoped for, stressed over for months. But then the "high" waned. I was forced to diagnose why I was feeling like a crinkled, shiny balloon where the helium was beginning to dissipate. A tinge of guilt floated alongside these feelings. We just won the states. Was I being ungrateful? No, I appreciated my teammates, coaches and every win. Was I moving on too quickly? No, or I wouldn't be pondering all of this.

After some thought, I came to a conclusion. It's not that I didn't welcome the achievement, it's just that for the first time I can remember, I realized there is more to life. At one time, I thought it couldn't get much better than winning the state championships, and then we won it in both sports and I thought, wow. Turns out, the cliché that the journey is better than the destination is true—at least, for that particular time in my life. I remember the burning in my chest after running hills at the end of every practice; the acidic taste which lined my mouth everytime I collided helmet-to-helmet with an opponent; the smell of grass after having been tackled; the sound of cheering and laughter on the bus ride home. The togetherness, leadership, and hard work throughout the four-month season proved the better experience than the presentation from the Governor of wooden plaques with gold lettering.

The dab of emptiness I felt after having hung the plaque on my wall did not arrive out of sadness or regret. Rather it came from place of contemplation. I gained extra space in my life very possibly to fill with something else beautiful and rewarding. Maybe it was actually an opportunity to find *more* joy in life. I just didn't know it yet.

During moments of emptiness, alarms don't sound nor do sirens blare. Rather, this deeper emptiness approaches like the wind through the evergreen trees. You know it's there because you see the tree move and hear the wind cut through the branches, but it takes a moment of silence to notice. And then this emptiness patiently stays, this cavern, living inside your soul until you enter, explore, and eventually come to some conclusions.

I enjoy carnivals, especially the kind which raise money for the volunteer fire company. The entire field or parking lot transforms into a fair with big and fast rides overnight—which should concern me. But the funnel cakes draw me in from a mile away, regardless. The candy apples sparkle in all the bright lights. Ping pong balls can be heard bounding off of goldfish bowls. The occasional bell rings from a strong man trying to win a teddy bear for his girl. I always ride the ferris wheel. And I walk into the fun house. Those two are a given for me. Anything else is just extra (or makes me dizzy and ill).

One night, I entered the funhouse with my tested and true strategy—no matter how tricky things look, just keep walking. Eventually, the exit will appear. Not that night. I should have thought better of it. The entire inside of the funhouse was constructed of flat, curved, round, and wavy mirrors. I kept inadvertently mashing my face into my own distorted reflection. After a considerable amount of time (might have been three minutes, but it felt like thirty), I began to wonder if I would get out before closing time. So I waited for someone else who paid for a ticket to walk in. I then followed them out.

It was a simple problem, in retrospect. But the whole experience took all of my concentration and, eventually, I needed help to get through.

Entering into deeper places, exploring strange emotions, and delving into what we call emptiness, can be very tricky, like walking into a fun house. You see yourself in different ways, sometimes distorted, sometimes not. The point is you see every angle of yourself. Sometimes that's not pretty. And sometimes, when you walk too far along the path, it is difficult to find your way out. Sometimes it even hurts. The stops, turns, and hidden entrances become deceptive or hard to navigate. That's when we need help to see our way through.

When we allow ourselves to probe into this emptiness, this "something missing," we really have only two options: diversion or exploration. Diversion simply means you fill the void with something else. Anything else. It could either be willfully ignoring the emptiness, or willfully self-medicating in some fashion (ignoring often proves to be the harder of the two). On the other hand, exploration means you are actively searching for the right thing to fill the void. You don't ignore the problem; rather, you are attempting to solve it. Diversion asks, "how can I quickly rid myself of this feeling?" Exploration asks, "why am I feeling this way?" in hopes of an answer. Diversion prioritizes expediency. Exploration prioritizes process. The diversion path will never truly fill the void which slowly crept in the night you first noticed.

Exploration will, but it requires humility and honesty with self—which is more difficult than we realize.

Diversions abound. Almost anything can be placed into this emptiness box, so naturally, we try to fill it with something...only to find it failed us, so we try something else. This cycle continues over time, usually measured in years. Eventually, however, it will become too heavy to carry. We are overtaken by the weight of the many failed attempts.

Emptiness crosses all socio-economic boundaries. This may seem counterintuitive, as poverty highlights the visible emptiness more readily than affluence. What many don't realize, however, is that the emptiness about which we speak has much more to do with deeper matters than money.

Poverty is foremost a lack of resources, and therefore, a lack of opportunity. Lack of opportunity causes a substantive sense of hopelessness, and indeed, of all things that hollow out an empty place in us, hopelessness tops the list. Exploration proves too painful for the hopeless, for the reality of their situation looks too bleak. Diversion is seldom an option, either, as the scant resources leave little room to fill the emptiness box. Poverty reveals much about emptiness.

But so does affluence. More money means more things and the more opportunity to fill emptiness with those things. They do so, only to find that flashy cars, manicured lawns, Ivy League schools, and beach houses have only the power to distract, and that distraction is only temporary. Remember, emptiness is patient. Resources allow those who have them to try to fill the little emptiness box with any number of things. And so they do—substance, success, sex, social standing, scholarship, stash, stocks—anything can be a diversion. Some of the deception of diversions lies in the fact that it claims to have the ability to fill the emptiness. It cannot. A beer doesn't make you happy forever, so you open another one. The feeling you got when you bought your first boat has dissipated, so you buy a new one to recapture the feeling. Maybe you decided the emptiness you feel is a result of a current relationship or your job, so you go back to Tinder, or Indeed. Rinse and repeat, and again sense the disappointment. Not that beers and boats and boyfriends are necessarily bad, they just aren't suited for the task of filling the emptiness box. The point of diversions is not to fill emptiness, but to rid *the sense of* emptiness and do so quickly.

Numerous repercussions are likely if the emptiness box finds no satisfaction, even if indirectly. Much like a catalyst. Catalysts accelerate a chemical reaction between other elements. The catalytic converter in a car contains platinum, which serves as a catalyst to change carbon monoxide into carbon dioxide. In other words, catalysts are not *the* element, rather a stimulant in the process between two elements. Emptiness can cause things in and of itself—for example, it can cause depression—but emptiness is also a catalyst. For instance, if depression hovers anywhere around emptiness, a molecular bond occurs. This bond can cause any number of dangerous reactions which endanger the host. Drug overdose and suicide are two, newsfeeds of which have been on a disturbing incline.

The sheer complexity of the whole human self cannot be overstated. University hospitals spend resources on the study of the human psyche, biochemistry, and biophysics. Certain cerebral functions are still being heavily researched—in fact, we know relatively little about the brain. Diseases and cures for those diseases comprise a large segment of biomedical research and development. Genetic coding largely eludes us. No two personalities are identical. Nurture versus Nature will always play a part in discussing behavioral sciences. Emotions, whether we like it or not, control most of our decision-making.

And then, in the middle of all the physical, emotional, psychological and technological breakthroughs, the *spiritual* part of us rolls in like a delivery truck coming down the driveway. You hear the brakes, the engine turn off, the thump of the package on the porch, the truck starting, and the motor vanishing into the distance. It's delivered and you can't deny it. It's here, and it's not going away.

So, too, the spiritual side of us, delivered to our front door, will require us to sign and accept. It is vital to the whole human self, a package with our name on the label.

The spiritual "us," so intricately related to the other parts of "us," escapes our reason and intellect to a degree because the sciences can only refer to it, point to it, and begin to explain it, but can't quite touch it. We call it metaphysical, or supernatural, because it is beyond our reach, beyond the realm of our senses. Those things are relegated to our souls. But we desperately want answers, because the sense of something "wholly other" than us will not go away.

There is a relationship between the spiritual component deep inside and the emptiness we feel. Both weigh on us. What is missing? Is that "something'" out there the answer we have sought, the solution to our emptiness? How can I fill the emptiness? God, are you there? Can you fill it? Where are you, anyway? These questions, all legitimate, seek to bring stability and wholeness deep within us in the midst of the restlessness. One thing is for sure: feeling like this for much longer ceases to be an option. But explaining it in terms of God seems like a cop-out.

But is it?

When contentment rescinds, restlessness climbs, intensifying the cry that there must be more. Irritable, discouraged, angry, and recluse, we keep searching. We strive to fill this emptiness as quickly as possible to avoid the cavernous aching. Our souls become "hangry."

Hangry is a made up word, a late addition to our English language. A legitimate addition, I might add, because I experience it frequently, and because I found it in the latest online dictionary. It is a combination of two other words, hungry and angry. I first learned of that term one day around noon when my son and I simultaneously became noticeably frustrated working on his truck. Attitudinal nose dive. Thrown wrench. Need food. Now. Hangry. And food works, changing our attitudes almost instantaneously. Funny how that works—how things change when you fill yourself with the right thing.

The other component to this emptiness finds company with dissatisfaction. The emptiness box is seemingly full, but the feeling of discontentment and dissatisfaction lingers. You have everything you could ask for, but still this emptiness haunts you. This, too, poses a problem. From everyone else's vantage point, what they see and hear, how they watch you interact with others, how they observe you solving problems, discussing sensitive subjects, what car you drive to work, what street you live on, you're doing fine. But you know you are not. They can't see inside, so how would they know? Your first instinct is to feel a growing shade of guilt. You think to yourself that maybe they are right in what they think. You should be fine, but you're not. And you can't come up with a perceptible reason why.

Stop here. The emptiness you feel was never intended to cause you guilt, but rather to get your attention. It was never meant to produce discouragement, but to point you to something more.

Long ago lived a woman in Sychar, a small desert town boasting a flowing well, an oasis of freshwater. The days were hot, and the walk to gather water was long and strenuous. Her swollen and sunburnt feet told the story of years trudging up the hill on the path to the well. With a wooden pole placed on her shoulders behind her neck, she balanced two large jars hung by ropes, one on the right and one on the left. Her gait slowed with every step. Squatting to set the jars along the side of the stone well, she rested for a moment. The walk back with jars full proved harder and harder every year.

Every day, she walked by herself to draw water from the town well. It's what women did. She seemed to have few friends, having trudged this path alone for years. Most women gathered water in the cool of the morning, chatting together as they did. Not so for her. Her past prohibited that. Broken, ostracized, and shamed by her promiscuous past, she dutifully filled the clay jars alone in the latter part of the morning when the sun seemed to laugh at those who had no shade. On this particular day, however, a strange man happened to be sitting beside the well. He struck up small talk upon her arrival. Her worn face told a story of the emptiness in her soul, as empty as the jars which sat on her shoulders.

The conversation turned toward deeper matters. Jesus's gentle demeanor drew her into this warm, somewhat therapeutic exchange. At the opportune moment, when things began opening up, Jesus made her an offer of healing and fulfillment. Having a knowledge of her shaded past, her current plight, and her sheer hopelessness, she looked at him with eyes that screamed "tell me more" but with a frown that said, "probably too good to be true." The offer had everything to do with filling empty things.

"If you only knew the gift God has for you and who you are speaking to, you would ask me, and I would give you living water" (John 4:10). That got her attention. Her thirst was real and of a different nature than that of the other women who arrived at the well earlier that day. Jesus addressed her thirst specifically. "Anyone who drinks this water will soon become thirsty again. But those who drink the water I give will never be thirsty again. It becomes a fresh, bubbling spring within them, giving them eternal life" (John 4:13-14).

When an offer is made which points to the undeniable emptiness deep inside, and a promise to fill it, people are bound to listen. If that promise to fill assures us an answer to the questions we have been asking, then our response may resemble hers.

"Please sir," the woman said. "Give me this water" (John 4:15).

On another occasion, Jesus spoke of the need to address this prevalent emptiness to a crowd. Droves of people were beginning to follow Jesus and adhere to his teaching by this point. He taught life-altering principles, articulated real issues, pointed out elephants in the room, and communicated to the soul, thereby appropriately challenging all those who had ears to listen. Jesus drew his teaching from common, everyday items, taking the object lesson and morphing it into something meaningful and hopeful in a way that everyone could understand. A great teacher takes complex things and teaches them simply. This day, Jesus used bread.

"I am the bread of life. Whoever comes to me will never be hungry again" (John 6:35). Simple enough.

It is hard to ignore the feeling of an empty stomach. You can be pushing a lawn mower, rolling dough, enjoying a movie, or hammering nails through shingles on a roof, but whatever you're doing, when hunger strikes, it persistently knocks until the activity temporarily halts, and the belly fills. Bread actually does quite a good job to settle hunger down, fill the void, get some carbs. I often feel bad for people who cannot eat bread. I feel less bad for people who choose not to.

Though bread is arguably the oldest prepared food on the planet, I think it is the most delicious, especially when sitting on a shelf in a bakery with all its sweet and flaky cousins. Just like bread satisfies the stomach, so the Bread of Life will satisfy the soul, filling the empty place with something suitable and adequate.

This profound emptiness is not just an ancient thing, however; it is a human thing. It always existed and always will. Long before Jesus arrived, a prophet named Isaiah penned words that addressed this deepest of needs. This particular writing is written in first person, as it is God talking, God drawing us into His presence.

"Is anyone thirsty? Come and drink—even if you have no money! Come, take your choice of wine or milk—it's all free! Why spend your money on food that does not give you strength? Why pay for food that does you no good? Listen to me, and you will eat what is good. You will enjoy the finest food. Come to me with your ears wide open. Listen to me and you will find life" (Isaiah 55:1-3).

Simply put, it's an invitation. Your soul continues to seek that which will satisfy the deepest part of who you are. It's free for the taking. The money you spend on filling, the time you invest in striving—pause that. Take a different approach. This passage makes something very clear: you *will* find fulfillment in God, if you accept the invitation.

Fill with what is "good" and find life. That is the invitation. It's an invitation to take the Living Bread, the Living Water, and fill the deepest and most alive place in you. Emptiness, it turns out, is just an invitation.

PAIN

"There is an ancient tribal proverb I once heard in India. It says that before we can see properly, we must first shed our tears to clear the way."

Libba Bray

"It hurts because it matters."

John Green

I stared out of my second floor window. That, in itself, was an accomplishment. Cold mist and dust particles from winter winds frosted the corners of the window panes. The snow, now melted off the driveway, lingered on the grass, creating a patchwork of whites and browns and greens. Water from the stream bubbled over the larger rocks as the melted snow pushed the volume higher than normal. Trees stood still as the winds rested from a month of overtime. And I saw a cardinal, its brilliant red the most vivid color through the glass before me.

I was glad to see the world outside still existed. After all, it had been weeks since I was on the first floor, even longer since I was outdoors. My world, at this time, was my bedroom, and my throne a rented medical chair.

So much happened between the time my doctor told me to have my wife drive me straight to the hospital and when the delivery truck brought the chair to my upstairs bedroom. My head spins thinking about it. Prior to the cardiologist's appointment, I noticed being out of breath only five minutes in on a treadmill. No worries. Just need to get in better shape. Then kettlebells in the driveway hurt my left shoulder. No worries. Just warm up more before lifting. I was determined to get into shape, so much so that I decided to go on a run, *Forrest Gump* style—run until you can't. I made it to the mailbox and decided to walk back. The next day, I shoveled three feet of snow, but felt a little queasy. I walked up and down the hill with the kids while they were sledding, but had to sit down.

My wife insisted I see a doctor, and so she called. They didn't like what they heard, so they required me to set up an appointment for a stress-echo. Two days later, I was on a treadmill hooked up to red, green, blue, yellow, black, and white wires.

The nurse said "stop" after only four minutes, when I usually go about thirteen, and then followed it up by telling me what a nice job I did. I wasn't buying it.

Sit down. Wait for the doctor. Don't leave. Drink some water. Wait for the doctor (repeated another four times). The doctor, whom I have never met before, finally arrived. He sat me in his office, showed me a computer monitor of my EKG, and sent me right to the hospital. Blocked arteries.

Cath lab at the hospital took a scan of my arteries. Results said stents were not an option due to the position and angles of the arteries. "Going to have to open you up for triple bypass," they said. Wow. I wasn't expecting all that. So I got a ride to the hospital.

Surgery the next morning. Early. That afternoon, ICU. I'm on all kinds of machines in more pain than I have ever felt before in my life. Almost a week of help from competent nurses. A few days before leaving, I watched the Super Bowl in the hospital room with my kids, brother, and sister.

Six days later I was in a brown leather chair with red and blue up/down buttons, staring at my bedroom wall. I couldn't move. Couldn't eat. Breathing hurt my ribs. And to top it off, I had appendicitis at the beginning of cardiac rehab.

The days seemed to get worse instead of better.

I pressed a button which would help me to my feet, but I always hoped it would jettison me into a better existence. Every day, I looked for that eject button.

That afternoon, however, I walked gingerly over to the window and placed my head on the cold glass, the cross-grilles placing a temporary dent on my forehead. The browns and grays of early March did little to convince me that I would ever get better. So I cried.

I'm not a cryer. But sometimes that's all there is to do. When our overloaded emotions merge with the numbness of our brains, the confluence brings flowing tears. Nothing to say, nothing to think, just pain. So, just tears.

Everyone says it's okay to cry—wives, parents, psychiatrists, ministers alike. I would agree, but just not at the moment when a teardrop slips past my nose and drops onto the window sill. No. At that moment, it doesn't feel okay.

But, alas, days did get better. Time and love. One foot in front of the other. Protein shakes. Short walks. Family time. Daily prayers. Rehab. And before long, things started coming back together again, like a time-lapse of a flower peeking from below the dirt and then blossoming with orange petals. It literally happened before I knew it. Next thing I knew, the six-month ordeal was over. Pain

PAIN

became a thing of the past, and I was glad to see it go. But the effects of that pain and the lessons learned turned out to be invaluable.

Pain brings more pain, and our whole self feels the hurt. Physical pain trips the emotional wire, while emotional pain trips the mental pain wire, and vice versa and so on. The signals cross and the currents which keep us balanced, healthy, and thinking well diverge and ground out. Depression sparks and the cycle of pain keeps manifesting in new ways. These are circular because we are whole selves, composed of mental, emotional, physical, and spiritual aspects. Therefore, pain affects us holistically.

Has physical pain ever triggered sadness in you? When the phone rings and the voice on the other side says that someone you love is lying lifeless on a hospital bed, has that ever caused your knees to buckle? When you walk into a bees' nest and six of them sting you, can you think rationally? Our whole self gets involved in pain. There is no hiding. Pain is a Rube Goldberg machine, the final act of which often leads to tears.

Pain is also an amplifier. The sounds of everyday life are drowned out when pain decides to strum the chord. The knob is permanently fixed at "loud." Grief causes us to sit. Evil causes us to curse. Loneliness causes us to imbibe. Insults cause us to ponder them until, sadly, we believe them to be true. Whoever said "sticks and stones will break our bones, but words can never hurt me" lives in a cave. Names will break our hearts, which is so much worse. The sounds of pain are just so loud.

Hope, though, has a finger on the volume control.

I see so much pain in the world. Pictures of starving families hurt at a deep level. Refugees evacuating a war-torn country stirs anger at the aggressors. And it all makes me feel powerless. Bullies choosing an innocent target saddens me, as I know the memory of it, for the one bullied, will last a lifetime. An athlete reading his name on the "cut list" after tryouts needs a hand on the shoulder, but often there is none to be found. Our hope in all this pain is that it will be okay in the end, that there will be something better right around the corner. We hope.

I see the faces of first-time visitors to an addiction recovery group. Shame dims the brightness in their eyes to a sullen gray, dulled from decisions made long ago. All of them wish that former choices could be retracted. Pain is now a part of their story, pain they caused to themselves and those closest to them. But here they are. And if you look a little closer, a sparkle appears in their eyes as they are welcomed, as they share the complete mess that defines their lives, and people clap, and want them to come back. That sparkle is called hope.

Pain also surfaces in other places. Injustice is a petri dish for pain. Let it sit too long, ignoring it, keeping it in the dark, and within a few days, the mold spores proliferate. I don't know about you, but something in the crevices of my inner self tell me that the pain people suffer from the actions of a transgressor is not only noticed, but will one day be made right. It has to.

We humans are fairly powerless to right every wrong, although we are fairly proficient at inflicting them. But there will be accountability because there is such a thing as justice. God promises that. God is concerned about wrongdoing, fairness, culpability, pain. When we look at the travesties committed in this world throughout history and the pain it has caused, the only hope we have is something more, something beyond us to help us make sense of this world.

God stands ready. His fairness is described as a plumb line. He will know who has a crooked wall. "The Lord demands accurate scales and balances;

he sets the standards for fairness" (Prov. 16:11). There is much peace in that.

As for the marginalized? Jesus had a soft spot for the destitute, poor, forgotten, hungry, sick. He pursued them at parties, bars, wheat fields, watering holes, deserts. He even instructed his hosts in a similar way. "But when you give a banquet, invite the poor, the crippled, the lame, the blind, and you will be blessed..." (Luke 14:12-13). Pain seems to draw Jesus's attention. I can get behind someone like that.

There is a good side to pain, however. Whether we want to admit it or not, pain has a purpose. On one hand, pain is a warning light on our dashboard to help us avoid that which is dangerous and life threatening. Hot—pull your hand away! Dangerous—run away! Sharp—drop it! Hurts—get an x-ray! Rude—walk away! We have all experienced these pains. But that is not the kind of pain which is our concern here.

On the other hand, the kind of pain that runs through our soul does something beneficial: it tells us we need fixing, and it won't let go until we get fixed. It tells us we need healing, and our emotional self won't move on until that process begins. It tells us that as resilient as we become through hardships, we can't do this alone. It tells us that there has to be more, and finding that can bring something needed more than any other thing in moments of pain—hope.

A few evenings ago, my wife and I dragged a few metal chairs together on the patio of a cafe, making a small circle to converse with friends. The four of us sipped simple coffees that night—no syrup, nor any other additive but frothed milk. Words seemed to ride the gentle winds, moving us to a place of warm conversation, the kind of night where deeper things flow. They began sharing with us moments of despair experienced over the last seven years. It seemed to them that as soon as one major thing resolved, another was introduced. Like pounding surf, just when you think it's okay to go out, another crashing wave sends you tumbling.

There was, however, something sweet in the vulnerability, the sharing of life. People were made to share, to celebrate, to grieve together, to help carry the burdens of those who can't carry it themselves. And there was something cathartic in their resolve throughout that season to hang onto God. It is good to cry out to God. *Please help. Please be with me.* Sometimes that's all we have. But often, as we come to realize, that's all we need.

A vector is a force which has the two characteristics of magnitude and direction. Many things have this unidirectional force, such as gravity, velocity (rockets and cars), and light rays. And, maybe, depression. In some ways, I think depression and desperation are vectors because they both have magnitude and direction. We feel it.

In geometry, vectors are represented by an arrow. Desperation and depression are vectors with its arrow pointing down, moving quickly toward the bottom of the tank. Suddenly we look around and we notice where we are. Maybe because it's a little darker. Maybe because we look at the soles of our shoes which have collected dust from living there too long. And we wonder how we got there.

But hope is also a vector. When the descending arrow has exhausted its runway, the hope vector bounces up, directing our attention to what is above. Darkness begins to dissipate as we see the vastness of the sky and its endless possibilities. There is magnitude and direction there, too. Hope raises our gaze northward, for when you are at the bottom, there is nowhere else to look but up. Our eyes squint due to the brightness of the light, having been accustomed to living in darkness a bit too long. But once our eyes adjust, our whole perspective changes. Hope's bright light penetrates even the clouds of pain which seek to hide it. And we notice.

Grief swelled that day in the small town of Bethany. It wasn't widespread like a natural disaster, touching every home with the sting of injury and death—but it was a bitter grief, nonetheless. Personal. Close. The worst kind. Bethany was a small town, the population only in the hundreds. When something tragic happens within the confines of such a small place, many are touched.

Mary and Martha, friends and followers of Jesus, loved their brother deeply. Seeing him lie there, listening to his shallow breaths—his forehead drenched with sweat, his skin chalky and pale—sent an ache through the tenderness of their souls. Illness wrecked his body and, eventually, in the presence of those who loved him, he succumbed to the cold winds of death.

Jesus arrived into town having heard the news and saw his friends and many others weeping upon hearing the news. The tears were understandable. After all, how could this have happened to the beloved Lazarus, so lively, a friend to all, and who had a full life ahead? Questions like that have been asked since the beginning of time.

Jesus responded to the news, to the grieving crowds, not with teaching, as was his custom. Instead, the scriptures said, "Jesus wept" (John 11:35).

Wept? The teacher, miracle worker, leader, wept? This one who had it all together? There were no words, no speeches, just tears. Yes, even Jesus felt pain. Pain spares no one. This response revealed more of his human nature than the best speech ever could have. Jesus felt deeply, just like you and I do. He felt the pain of seeing dear friends cry. He felt the sadness of someone he loved lying lifeless on a bed of straw. I love how the story ended, strange and miraculous as it was. Jesus demonstrated power beyond anything anyone had seen to this point. This miracle, though, would top them all. He walked slowly to the cave tomb of his recently deceased friend. Along with being sad, the Bible says Jesus was deeply troubled in his spirit, feeling an acute sense of anger along with the sadness. With words that carried the emotions of a full heart and the thundering power from heaven, Jesus spoke life back to the lifeless body of Lazarus. Sometimes painful emotions must precede satisfying solutions. Passion, after all, is the best motivator for making a difference.

PAIN

Jesus was no stranger to pain. Once, soon after he and his disciples left the comforts and camaraderie of the Seder dinner, Jesus's last supper, they walked to a grove of olive trees. They had congregated there often over the last three years. Jesus's mind raced, knowing that within the hour, unspeakable things would begin. He would be beaten with hardwood clubs, whipped with leather laces, the ends of which were tied with bone chips and weighted with lead, and then flogged thirty-nine times. Then, he would have to endure a makeshift trial, where he would be found guilty. His forehead would bleed profusely due to thorns being tapped into his skin. Death by crucifixion, after that. He knew all this, so he stopped to do the only thing he knew to do—cry out to God.

He asked his disciples to do the same while he found a solitary place where he might pray. "He walked away, about a stone's throw, and knelt down and prayed, 'Father, if you are willing, please take this cup of suffering away from me. Yet I want your will to be done, not mine'" (Luke 22:41-42). A few verses later, it describes the anguish. "He prayed more fervently, and he was in such agony of spirit that his sweat fell to the ground like great drops of blood" (Luke 22:44).

While Jesus prayed, his inner suffering increased, the weight of the world about to be placed on his shoulders. That's a heaviness I have yet to experience. I hope I never do. The account tells us that it was, in fact, so heavy, that angels came to his side in order to strengthen him. To make matters worse, the disciples he asked to stay up and pray with him, to not leave him alone, were later found sleeping. They had abandoned him.

Jesus did not desire to suffer in this way. No one does. But he trusted in the nearness, the tenderness, and the sheer love God had for him. Even if that meant he had to endure unspeakable pain.

Before that last night, Jesus traveled to many towns, teaching, healing, and serving the people who lived there. He knew the pain of the individuals, saw its effect, and addressed it. One such day, after teaching some rather difficult subjects, Jesus spent some of his time praying over the people. His prayer ended abruptly, and then, with all the compassion he could muster, he made an invitation to everyone listening. Jesus, having known past and present pain, and the suffering to come, invited us to himself—especially when we experience such pain. The fact that he understood human suffering made his invitation to us so much more meaningful, relevant, needed.

"Come to me, all you who are weary and carry heavy burdens, and I will give you rest" (Matt. 11:28). Jesus's approach was one of gentleness, understanding, kindness, patience, compassion. His offer is rest—the number one and age-old requisite for healing. To accept his offer is to invite wholeness once again to our physical ailments, mental anguish and emotional scars. Jesus is effective to heal the pain, for the ointment he offers is a spiritual compound, a salve that reaches beyond the skin to the soul.

Jesus takes all our brokenness, all our pain, all our lostness, and says, "Behold I am making all things new" (Rev. 21:5). He later states his intention to wipe every tear from our eyes, being that the place where he resides at this very moment is devoid of death, sorrow, crying, and pain. These things are gone forever. But for now, we have to endure what painful experiences meet us—just as he did. Jesus told the disciples while sitting in that upper room, during that last supper, "I have told you all this so that you may have peace in me. Here on earth you will have many trials and sorrows. But take heart, because I have overcome the world" (John 16:33).

Yes, we will have trouble. But yes, we will have Jesus.

Yet listen, there's more, lest you think that Jesus is only concerned about your future. He cares about you right now, wherever you are, whatever you are going through, no matter the circumstance. To demonstrate the unequivocal nature of that personal concern, God does something so startling, so miraculous, we are left speechless: God collects all your tears and places them in a jar for safe keeping. Did you hear that? God takes this saline mixture that falls from your eyes, born from a pain so great, so all-encompassing that it "had" to come out—and he stores them. "You keep track of all my sorrows. You have collected all my tears in your bottle. You have recorded each one in your book" (Psalm 56:8). Imagine it. Not only does God collect your tears, because they came from *you*, but he also notes in his journal why you shed them on that dark and cloudy day. It is recorded because he loves you and keeps tabs on how you are really doing. No pretense. No hiding. Just the real you. The honest you. God *knows*. And he will continue to love. So none of your pain goes unseen, nor wasted. Astounding.

I don't pretend to know what other people go through. I can, however, feel some of what they feel. After all, I have had my share of broken hearts, shattered dreams, dashed promises. Our humanness means pain will be a very real part of our existence. I don't like it any more than you do. One thing I can do is point you to that "something more," to a God who cares so deeply for you that he weeps, who cherishes you so notably that he keeps your tears, who invites you to come into his arms when desperation has settled on you. God will not only get you through, but, like a collector who restores valuable items, he takes broken things back to his workshop. He will restore your beauty, your usefulness, your hope, bringing happiness and healing, the way one might take an old rusty Radio Flyer wagon and begin the work of refurbishing until the brilliant red paint and vivid white lettering once again return.

REMORSE

"My guiding principle is this: guilt is never to be doubted."

Franz Kafka

"Every saint has a past and every sinner has a future."

Oscar Wilde

*L*ooking back on my early teenage years, I find my mind drifting to several incidents, innocuous as they may have been, which remind me that age thirteen is not typically known for brilliance.

On the outskirts of town, a vacant indoor tennis facility stood in the middle of a parking lot overgrown with protruding green foliage in each of its cracks, forming a sort of maze to which the side entrance was the finish line. Someone, at some point, broke the hinge where the padlock tried to keep thirteen-year-old boys out. In our developing minds, an abandoned building plus a broken lock was equal to an invitation. One of us turned the rusted handle with enough strain on our face to loosen the rust, while two others pushed the door open until the creaking hinges stopped us. What we found was somewhere between a giant clubhouse and a hidden treasure.

Other than dust accumulated over years of neglect, the floor looked new. Dozens of tennis balls were strewn around the courts, left from the last tennis lesson a few years since. The walls and ceiling showed no signs of disrepair, no rust, no holes in the tin roof, no sign of any threat caused by the latest snowfall. The only oddity was the rhythmic tapping of branches off a black walnut tree blowing in the wind. Time to check the equipment.

A flick of the switch on the wall immediately to the left of the entrance lit the whole facility. Electricity! Our gawking eyes spotted an electric tennis ball machine resembling a small cannon sitting on one of the courts. Maybe, just maybe, it still shoots. A simple plug into the wall would tell a tale of either immense entertainment or disappointment—or, of course, electrocution. Someone was chosen to test the plug, someone who either knew enough to assess the safety of such action, or someone who was oblivious to the risks and dangers of AC current electrical shock. Either way, it was time to test. He pushed the three-prong plug into the socket. No sparks, a dull thud. Then, a ball shot out toward the side door. Yes!

Being baseball players and not tennis players, we determined it best, after some entrepreneurial thinking, to bring not tennis rackets, but aluminum bats to the facility. We realized that we discovered our own secret batting cage. From then on, we established one goal: become good hitters and make the travel team. A few laughs and high-fives later, we planned to meet the next day.

Finding this wonderful personal batting facility in itself was not a thing of remorse, though perhaps it should have been. Last time I checked, breaking and entering is unlawful, but at the time, I didn't feel bad about it at all. Remorse only entered the picture half a year later, when, having felt the need for extra batting sessions on the weekends, I "borrowed" the tennis ball machine for a long weekend to hit the balls in my backyard. That worked for about two days, and then the machine just stopped working. In my shed, tinkering with the switch, a sense of remorse fell over me. I realized that my self-seeking, haphazard, and short-range planning wrecked something special. I stole the machine, then broke the machine. My friends began to inquire, so I stayed on the slippery slope I created for myself, taking the fastest and easiest way out: I lied. Insisted I didn't take it.

Remorse is a gnawing feeling that arises from an acute sense of guilt for a past wrong—or in my case, wrongs. I was self-absorbed at that time; my thoughts only centered on myself, my desires, my advancement in a passing dream to play in the big leagues. I may have stolen the tennis cannon, but right along with it I stole the fascination, discovery, and perhaps even the dreams of one or two of the other kids hoping to make the travel team in the coming spring. Such honest thoughts, however, come from hindsight, maturity, and well, that gnawing. I never forgot my actions, and I've always felt bad about how I handled myself at that time. But time moved on and within six more months the whole thing was forgotten. For some of us baseball continued into travel leagues and high school. For others, lacrosse, girls, and academic interests moved to the forefront. All these years later, I still feel a tinge of regret, never having come clean, much less apologize.

The root of the word remorse stems from the Latin "mordere" which means "to bite." So remorse truly does gnaw. Again and again. Like a swarm of carpenter bees on fresh two-by-fours. My wife bought a carpenter bee catcher at a craft show in order to trap the furry black-and-yellow insects.

They had, by that time, bored several dozen perfectly round holes into the wooden railing of my deck, now in need of repair. I have always wondered why they don't call them "demolition bees."

The gnawing effect of remorse can be just as damaging. How much of the wooden frame inside of us has been gnawed down by remorse? Is there a way to rid and repair?

Remorse takes something from us, and sometimes leaves a trace of venom in its wake—like the sting left from the mandibles of a red ant, or a living room infested with fleas. The accumulation of such bites causes us to have to address them. We spray insect bite medication on them to help stop the itching. Or scratch the tiny little red marks scattered along our ankles until they bleed. Either way, the itching stops...for a time. Remorse, in a similar fashion, can't be left alone. How we tend to it matters. How many times have we felt remorse over the years only to let tangle up our insides, requiring a counselor to painstakingly unwind it? How many times have we medicated it, only to find that the next morning, it still aches? How, then, do I eliminate remorse once it bites?

Remorse is so hard because it is the byproduct of something we did to ourselves. No one forced remorse on us. We chose it. In other words, we never intended to acquire remorse. We took that risk of acquisition the minute we made a morally wrong decision. The hard part, however, is that we have to admit that we did something wrong in the first place to begin healing. Remorse, then, is linked to choice. A choice is made, and then, whether immediately or not, we regret it.

But I am not talking about regret. Remorse differs from regret, though many people use the two terms synonymously. Regret, in a similar way to remorse, also results from a past decision, a path you wish you could backpedal, a choice you wish you could withdraw. The difference lies in the fact that remorse always has a moral component to it. Regret may not. I regretted having to wake up three dozen middle school students on a weekend beach retreat to see the sunrise, but that was not remorse. I regretted passing on a 5-speed Ford SHO in perfect condition, but that was not remorse. I regretted volunteering to be in the dunk tank on a windy, 58 degree day, but that was not remorse. That's not to say that the lines between regret and remorse don't blur at times. I am forced to consider the difference because, unfortunately, I think I tend to struggle with regret more than most.

Let's now go back to a fourteen-year-old boy (a year older, a year smarter). A neighbor friend—I think she had a crush on me—asked me to accompany her to a banquet at the private school she attended. I saw no harm. We had been friends and neighbors for years—she was a part of the neighborhood crew who often went sledding together in the winter and played "kick the can" in the summer. So I agreed.

For the better part of three weeks, I planned, albeit reluctantly, to go. The reluctance mainly stemmed from the fact that I didn't do so well in crowds back then. Nerves and lack of conversational skill usually got the best of me. Yet, in spite of those shortcomings, I planned to go with her.

Until the night before. Maybe I lacked the desire to push myself past my insecurities. Maybe I didn't want her to think I was suddenly her boyfriend. Maybe I didn't have the fortitude to keep my word. Maybe all of the above. Whatever it was, I canceled on her the night before the event over the phone. A few days later, regret mixed with remorse like orange juice after having just brushed my teeth. She was a friend and I really let her down. Feeling awful, I promised myself I won't ever do that again.

We can regret career decisions, paint colors, stock choices, menu items, or a vote. We add *remorse* to the dish when we embezzle, vandalize, steal, cheat, slander, and default on our promises. We regret when we speak bluntly merely because it crept to the front of our mind, disregarding sensitivity to the timing of that comment. We accrue remorse when we don't say sorry afterward. We regret when we root for the wrong team. Remorse appears when we lose our partner's savings account over it.

This begs the question: from where does remorse come? It's a curious question. We are not taught to feel remorse, yet, like a two-year-old who says "no" to Mama, it just shows up. Remorse has an origin, a source. And that matters.

I enjoy occasional social media time watching what some deem rather strange—survival in the animal kingdom. Maybe it's the chase, or the fight, or the escape, or the infrequent victory by an underdog that fuels my competitive nature. The same thought surfaces each time: a stark difference between animals and humans is the lack of remorse. The alligator cares little for how beautifully crisp the lines of a zebra wrap around its body while lapping water from the muddy pond. The cheetah is heartless when a young antelope gets separated from its kin. The snow owl feels nothing for the furry, fattened rabbit warming itself in the sunshine. The reason? Animals have two goals: to survive and reproduce, both of which keep them highly motivated. While some animals show more signs than others of the ability to protect and nurture their species, remorse will never be part of their emotional repertoire.

It is different for me and you. We as humans feel something on a deeper level and on a higher plane. *Deeper* means there is a palpable element to it. *Higher* means there is a moral aspect to it. A sense of right and wrong is superglued to the human soul. That is why every culture, from the highly technological cities to the primitive agrarian farmlands, from the Silicon Valley to the Amazon River Valley, concur on several behaviors. There is general agreement worldwide as to the rightness and wrongness of thievery, first-degree murder, and spousal infidelity. That sense must be generated somewhere. So, in a very strange way, remorse points us to something more, something out there that speaks to our soul, calling us to be our best selves.

While people can debate the veracity of each individual right and wrong, no one can debate what one feels. Feelings are real and they belong to us, like it or not. An honest look through the crafted lenses of our soul reveals the reality of remorse. We know when something is off, out of whack. No one can escape a sense of fairness. Ask yourself:

when was the last time you thought something to be unfair? Bet it wasn't that long ago. This acute sense of fairness dances with a legitimate sense of justice. It is so because of a moral law which resides in all humans. As a matter of fact, it is moral law which prompts the question of remorse's origin. Logic, then, concludes that where there is a moral law, there must be a moral lawmaker.

Here's the catch. Remorse is sticky. When I say or do something that yields remorse, it is hard to remove. Remorse is the pine sap after breaking a green branch off a tree—only this time, all the chemicals in the world fail to expunge it. The morning alarm goes off in hopes that this remorse had somehow vanished under the moonlit night. But no, you awoke with it still in you. What we truly want is the removal of remorse. We want a company to come in and clean up the toxic spill from that derailed freight train. But you are powerless to remove it. There must be something more, something with the capacity to rid the pine sap, a solvent to pour over the stickiness and watch it melt away.

The disciples and the many other followers of Jesus began their journey with him on the Mount of Olives. People arrived in droves, having traveled hours, even days with kids in tow to hear the teacher. They carried canes, blankets, and flatbread made the day before. Quietly, the crowd nestled onto their hillside spot, listening to every word, hushing the children and others who whispered too loud. He taught at great lengths on many critical and pertinent issues of daily life and faith. During that time, Jesus specified a powerful and helpful way to pray, a way which would capture the essence of how to begin and end every day. Most of us know this prayer as "The Our Father." I find it quite interesting that the most prayed prayer in history contains the phrase, "and forgive us our trespasses..." (Matt. 6:12). Embedded in the middle of that short prayer is the request for forgiveness. Jesus makes it an assumption, a forgone conclusion that we all need forgiveness. The need for forgiveness and the assumption that God listens to us is yet another way that Jesus points us to God.

On the very last night of Jesus's life, before his pending execution, the twelve disciples gathered with Jesus on the second floor of a nondescript home in Mount Zion, just outside of the old Jerusalem walls. The floorboards, smooth from years of walking, led to a room where rugs, stuffed pillows, and a short-legged table waited for guests.

Being the Jewish holiday of Passover, the owner of the home presented the traditional Seder meal to them. Seeing this as a sacred occasion, and his last opportunity to serve those he dearly loved, Jesus made this time count.

One by one, the disciples walked into the home. The Passover meal would soon begin. Jesus followed the prayers, readings, and protocol of the Seder meal. There would be matza, lamb chop, an egg, bitter herbs. Everyone together would wash hands, hear the telling of the Passover story, sing songs of praise. Jesus, however, used this opportunity to morph the traditional Passover order by adding his own touch, his own meaning. He broke the bread and handed it to his disciples, citing that this represented Jesus's body, broken for all of them. They did not as of yet understand its full meaning. Then, right before the second cup of wine, Jesus imparted words which would give new, fresh, relevant and memorable meaning to this feast.

"He took a cup of wine and gave thanks to God for it. He gave it to them and said, 'Each of you drink from it, for this is my blood, which confirms the covenant between God and his people. It is poured out as a sacrifice to forgive the sins of many" (Matt. 26:27-38). Communion remembers the utter need for and significance of forgiveness. Taking the bread and the wine is meant to remind its partakers that remorse is not permanent, that there is a solvent which immediately removes the sap, that you don't have to fear waking up to the gnawing of remorse.

No one knew remorse more than "her." Nameless, this woman carried with her the humiliation of public disgrace. She was to be stoned. Her executioners? Citizens of the very town she knew so well. They lived on her street, or encountered her at the market. Some may have even acquired her services. In hopes they wouldn't be found out, the simplest solution was to join the execution squad.

Prostitutes, according to the law, would not only not be tolerated, but be put to death. I wonder if, when facing the mob of angry eyes and furrowed brows, a question or two arose in her mind. *How did I get here? Why did I make the choices I made? Is there any way to undo what was done? Was it worth it? Is this how I will die?*

The crowd dragged her to Jesus the teacher, the one with uncanny wisdom and all the answers. Here she sat in front of Jesus, shamed, guilty, desperate. Here Jesus sat, looking at the dirt around his feet, drawing pictures with his finger. The crowd broke the silence.

"'This woman was caught in the act of adultery. The law of Moses says to stone her. What do you say?'" (John 8:4-5).

How would Jesus respond to a pack of angry wolves bent on spilling her blood? It says he kept drawing in the dust. He knew they were out to trap him. If Jesus advises the mob to let her go, then he could be accused of not following the law. If he suggested they kill her, then maybe he lacked the mercy of which he spoke so often.

This time Jesus broke the silence. "All right..." said Jesus.

All right? Is that all he had to say? There was nothing "all right" about this situation. A lady was going to die. But another sentence followed.

"...But let the one who has never sinned throw the first stone!" (John 8:7).

Minutes passed. Nothing to be heard but crickets.

The text says that, one by one, everyone in that accusatory mob walked away until only Jesus and the woman were left in the middle of the crowd who had gathered to hear Jesus teach. Awkward silence followed. The crowds waited to see what happened next. Shame kept the woman voiceless, but the silence was broken once again as Jesus initiated a dialogue laden with tenderness and mercy of which Jesus often modeled.

He looked into her eyes, then stood up and said to the woman, "Where are your accusers? Didn't even one of them condemn you?"

"No, Lord," she said.

And Jesus said, "Neither do I. Go and sin no more" (John 8:10-11).

There was deliverance that day. Remorse was reversed. Grace won the day. Turns out that the "something more" is a some*one*. Jesus forgives. If you don't believe me, look at what Jesus said on the cross regarding the scoffing onlookers, the misguided religious leaders, and the emotionless executioners. "Father forgive them for they don't know what they are doing" (Luke 23:34).

I don't know about you, but I could use that kind of grace. Removing remorse is akin to freedom. A fresh start, a new beginning, a clean slate. Everyone longs for that at some point. We are ultimately helpless to remove remorse, but Jesus is ultimately help*ful*, in the truest sense of that word. It says of God, written in the first century by a man named Paul, "He is so rich in kindness and grace that he purchased our freedom with the blood of his Son and forgave our sins" (Eph. 1:7).

Sounds really good about right now. Without forgiveness, without expunging remorse, things spiral hopelessly downhill. White lies pile up and turn darker. Bad intentions mount and gain strength with each day. Greed costs more than money as our souls drain. Jealousy will burn our hearts down. Cheating lands you in the "L" column all day long. The things people don't know, those things deep inside that we tend to keep covered up, unseen or unheard by others, untold by us, and unconfessed, are usually what keeps us awake at night. Without forgiveness, remorse hovers like an evening fog on the New England coast, causing us to search for bearings, for hope.

Forgiveness is the lighthouse, pushing its signals through the density of the fog to tell you where to anchor safely. Jesus is the harbormaster who tells you to dock, and take the load off once and for all.

BLESSING

"Gratitude lifts our eyes off the things we lack so we might see the blessings we possess."

Max Lucado

"This is a wonderful day, I have never seen this one before."

Maya Angelou

I planted my elbows on the papers strewn across my desk and buried my fists into my cheeks like I was in the middle of a prize fight. Too many decisions were on my mind, too much weight on my shoulders, piles of papers and endless deadlines. I just needed one quiet moment to think—and perchance eke out a sensible prayer.

A familiar train whistle sounded, tempting me to purchase a one-way outbound ticket. But, alas, the sound was not a real train, but my text tone. I was glad for it, however. Few things as simple as a text tone can jolt you out of a trance like that. I think it works even better than a ringing phone. A name appeared on top of the queue alongside the blue dot of an unread message—a longtime friend. "You want a bagel or coffee I can bring over? Hope you're doing well."

Somehow this simple, two-sentence text—one question and one wish—found significance in that moment. It was exactly what I needed. A sign that someone was wishing me well. A true blessing. I wasn't hungry and I was already brimming with caffeine, but the fact that he knew some of my struggles and he was thinking of me was like fairy dust sprinkled over my morning. That text set a different course for the rest of my day.

The simple act of reaching out to one another addresses a multiplex of experiences and challenges which life brings. The feelings, friendship, and familiarity which we share with one another creates a high rise of care, concern, and compassion—if we let it. Reading between the lines is necessary. When they say, "Would a coffee help?" they really mean, "Been thinking about you." When they say, "How about a pastry?" they really mean, "Sometimes a break to eat something sweet makes the day go better," or, "I know what you have been carrying the last month or so. I said a prayer for you." Something as simple as, "Anything I can do?" can send the message, "You know I'm always here for you. Hang in there."

When I got one of those veiled messages of love, I couldn't help but notice a slight smile emerge against my will.

I found that text to be well within the confines of a true blessing. And it pointed to an even greater blessing: that of friendship.

I believe blessings like these are more commonplace than people are able or even willing to notice. We can get caught up in our own hardships, which dims the daylight just enough to make the landscape look black. It often takes a simple thing to smack us back into the golden hour where colors are vibrant, deep, and dreamlike. In that vivid place of friendship and care, we revisit the unwritten list in our hearts of those things which are truly most important. We get a little closer to what "blessing" really means.

There is great value associated in gaining a better understanding of overused terms. Words carry undertones of meaning which, depending on our culture and vocabulary, can vary drastically. "Blessing" is such a word. Blessing can be defined as a special favor, or a gift which brings happiness, or even goodness bestowed by God. But to describe it from experience, we mostly *feel* a blessing when we encounter it. Words can only do so much.

The blessing of relationships, of having others with whom to do life, top most people's list. The mom who makes a favorite hot meal when her adult child comes back for a visit. The teacher who cared enough to express belief in a student's skill. A child next to their father's hospital bed, sharing small talk, watching the game on a tiny TV hanging from the ceiling. The gathering of family and friends crowding around the corner of your kitchen, hidden, waiting for you to walk in the front door on your 50th birthday. The gentle voice of a spouse when a day seems to unravel. Yes, people top the list of blessings.

Those, however, are not the only things etched on our "blessings" list. A blue sky after a week of rain. A rosebush once thought dead sprouts a bloom. You walk in a convenience store reading a sign that reads "free coffee today." Somehow, you actually had a ten dollar bill in your pocket to offer a homeless man. An all-time favorite plays through your radio on the way home, so you crank the volume and sing along. The moonlit waves crash into the sand and trickle onto your toes as you gaze upon the reflection. Yes, many things can be seen as blessings. They are everywhere.

I once took a group of young adults and high school students on a two-week trip to a remote part of Guatemala. An orphanage needed laborers for construction and programs for the children. Part of that time required us to hike into villages where the homes were constructed of cinder-block walls, dirt floors, and open window frames. Chickens ran in and out of the house like a time-lapse video of a busy train station. Despite the language barrier, the villagers smiled often and waved repeatedly. Kindness and warmth were felt in every step. One more unanticipated characteristic proved noteworthy—they were thankful. Very much so.

While walking toward the village center, a few of us were hailed from the road and invited into a home. A sun-browned man in a dirty, white, button-down shirt, faded jeans, and a torn straw hat waved us toward him. His missing teeth whistled words and sentences. Whiskers illuminated his smile. We waved back and walked toward his house. His wife scurried around the kitchen, which was no more than an open fire in the middle of the house. Scant white and yellow flowers hung with wire on the exterior walls, adding a vibrant corsage to the gray block. The only mutually understood word bellowed three or four times from that gentleman, while smiling and catching eyes with us travelers, was, "Cafe! Cafe! Cafe!" He yelled the word over and over, while holding a tin cup in the air. Never have I once turned down an offer for coffee, and won't start now. We partook, smiled, and made genuine eye contact while sipping the freshly picked and roasted coffee. A few of us managed to serve up a little conversation as well. All of us drank from tin cups stained with rust from subtropical humidity and years of generosity.

What stayed with me, however, was their joy, their sheer pleasure at the sight of guests sitting in their home, shooing away the chickens and savoring the steaming java. They exuded gratitude. Thankful for everything they had, seemingly unaware of what they didn't. They had each other, coffee, and chickens, and thought they were rich. What I carried in my backpack may have been worth more than all of what they possessed. They hadn't noticed. Everything to them was a blessing.

There is just no way to see a blessing without the lens of gratitude. Gratitude brings into focus the magnificent and the mundane, the everyday things that are heard and healed, sensed or seen, told or touched, which constitute a day of blessings. A blessed life, then, is one where we recognize blessings for what they are—things that make us happy we are alive.

"Blessing" is a rich word pointing us beyond ourselves to something more. Think about it. Where does the word "thanks" go when it rolls off our tongue? Is your "thanks" heard in the absence of anyone else around? Maybe you just received a bonus. Or you avoided a car accident. You saw that an old friend tried to call. An unexpected rebate check came through the mail. The person you have interest in left a note for you in your cubicle. These things cause you to blurt out "thanks."

Gratitude should not be a sentiment that stays inside and grows or diminishes depending on our attitude and circumstances. It should appear in all circumstances at some point, like a butterfly on a black-eyed susan, gently landing but flapping its wings so as to catch your attention. When I practice gratitude, anxiety and depression decrease; positivity and happiness increase. Sad to say, the opposite is true in my life as well. Therefore, I have to discipline myself to always be thankful. Gratitude chases away negativity, comparison, and worry. Living with that kind of mindset—of gratitude, whether or not another person is watching—will pay dividends to our mental and emotional health. If you don't believe me, Google the effects of gratitude. Staggering.

It seems to me that if there is actually something for which to be thankful, there must be someone to thank. Often, the little blessings come not so much from another human being, but another place altogether. Someone is behind the blessings in your life and deserves to get credit. God is tapping on your shoulder through every blessing you receive. Sooner or later, "thanks" has to go somewhere—and God is ready to accept it.

Many thousands of years ago, a scribe recorded an ancient blessing spoken over a whole nation. The words were so powerful, straightforward, and poetic, that it eventually became the most famous recorded blessing of all time, spoken over individuals and crowds for millennia.

"The LORD bless you and keep you;

The LORD make His face shine upon you,

   And be gracious to you;

The LORD lift up His countenance upon you,

   And give you peace." (Numbers 6:24-26 New King James Version)

Upon closer examination of the words, the poetry reveals the same blessing stated in three different ways. Blessing, then, means God's smile, God's favor, and, by extension God's protection (grace and peace). In other words, God notices you, meets you where you are, and brings that which you desperately need—his presence. Ancient blessings depicted God's direct involvement in an individual's life and projected a special future for the ones being blessed. All spoken and written blessings henceforth include the power and passion displayed within this frame.

To notice a blessing sparks a desire in humans to speak in some way, in much the same way we cheer when our favorite team scores a game-winning run, or when we discover a historical fact that changes our entire perspective. We say, "Awesome!" "Wow!" "Interesting!" "Great!" And then, hopefully—"thank you." It is the "thank you" which gently points to God, like the delicate red arrow always pointing north when you pull the compass from your pocket.

The power of Earth's magnetism intrigues us, and so does the draw of an unexpected blessing. It makes me come to grips with the best of thoughts, that God is nearer than I might imagine; that God sees, feels, and tends to me; that God has my best interests in mind. Blessings are a wink from God, offered to everyone, that we might be attentive to his goodness. Everyday blessings, then, point to the One who blesses.

Jesus sat on a tree branch a stone's throw from the crowd. He needed space to think creatively.

Ideas needed to percolate. Jesus needed to decide how he would begin his sermon before he taught the throngs of people who had gathered today. This particular sermon would be his longest and most memorable—it would overflow with everyday wisdom. But first, he needed to find an adequate beginning point, a story or catchy phrase to hold their attention. He needed a hook to keep people turning the pages of their attention span, expanding their enthusiasm and increasing their hope. He paced, threw stones, and looked up to the sky. Sometimes, creativity is hard to come by.

The introduction also needed to be splashed with the element of encouragement and positivity, for the days were hard. Life in ancient Israel presented more adversity than advantage. The Romans demanded steep taxation, money the farmers could not afford. Governors and centurions treated the Israelites as though they were lesser people. There seemed to be no chance of ever getting ahead. Poverty was a way of life.

A thought hit him. After asking himself what the people needed, the inspiration shot like an arrow into his thinking. He started with a fascinating word: "blessed."

Do you want to know how to be blessed? Do you want to see the eventuality of a blessed life? Are you interested in God's view on the blessings he bestows? Yeah, Jesus thought. Let's start there.

"Blessed are the poor in spirit..., blessed are those who mourn..., blessed are the gentle..., blessed are those who hunger and thirst for right things..., blessed are the merciful..., blessed are the pure in heart..., blessed are those who work toward peace..., blessed are those who are ridiculed and hurt for living according to God's ways" (Matt. 5:3-10).

He missed no one. The list included everyone. The possibility of living a blessed life and securing an even more blessed life floated into the ears of eager listeners. Furthermore, there were promises associated with this kind of blessing. They will be satisfied, comforted; they will be shown mercy and will see God's hand clearly at work; they will be called God's own children and receive an inheritance of some kind. It sounded too good to be true, but also too true to be ignored or dismissed as a pie-in-the-sky, idealistic, positive-thinking type speech. The kind with content but no substance. So this comprehensive, promise-filled list was worth believing.

Jesus's lifelong passion was to bless others. It was a central part of how he might change individuals. He wanted to tell them they are loved. Tell them they are gifted. Tell them they are valuable. He wanted to change the individual, create a space in their souls for hope, and change the world. After all, that's what blessings do.

Once, during one of Jesus's teaching opportunities, the disciples rebuked an assemblage of children and their parents for disrupting the teacher. Customary to the time and place where they lived, a rabbi was not to be interrupted without forewarning. But Jesus was different. He loved children and desired that all come near to him. Here were children being children, chasing each other in the streets, kicking up dust, laughing and squealing just as kids do. He didn't mind an occasional infant crying for want of milk. Parents kept their kids close by so as to not miss the blessing when Jesus called their name.

When Jesus noticed that the disciples were treating the children with disapproval, the Scripture passage says he became angry. Not at the children, but at the disciples. Funny that such a strong word was used to describe Jesus's response. But it reveals the nature and importance to him of such an opportunity. The disciples missed it entirely. They missed the blessing of shrill happiness in the tiny voices, the smiles of missing teeth—and they nearly missed the opportunity to allow their master to lay hands on the little ones and bless them, to project on them a special future, to declare over them God's goodness. "Let the children come to me and don't stop them!" (Mark 10:14). Two verses later, "Then he took the children in his arms and placed his hands on their heads and blessed them" (Mark 10:16). So simple, profound, transformative.

The disciples sat around a campfire, smoke filling their eyes at every gust of wind. Breakfast consisted of fish, fish, and more fish. The morning proved quiet, the events of the prior week having yet to settle in their minds. Jesus left it that way. Sometimes it is okay to sit, think, enjoy the presence of others, and savor a good meal. However, Jesus knew the time was approaching that he would have to leave. His leaving would inaugurate a new age where people would pick up where he left off.

The entirety of Jesus's ministry centered on love. Love God and love others. Live that way, and people would be sure to make a difference. Do you know what the last thing Jesus did for the disciples while still with them on earth? He blessed them. "Then Jesus led them to Bethany, and lifting his hands to heaven, he blessed them" (Luke 24:50).

I always wondered what that blessing entailed. I wish we had a transcript as to what was said.

Old Testament blessings, of which Jesus was very familiar, contained elements of love, spoken affirmation, and unique encouragement. These blessings promised the nearness of God, his protection and provision. There is no doubt to me the blessing included all of those elements. "You are loved!" I can imagine Jesus saying. "You are doing great! You are using your gifts and abilities well! People are changing! Keep going! Don't give up! May God be with you! May God strengthen you! May God bring you blessing after blessing!"

I have found it periodically difficult to maintain a lifestyle of gratitude. Sometimes it's just plain hard, given current circumstances. I guess that is why some categorize thankfulness and gratitude as a discipline.

How about for you? Are you able to peel the wallpaper off of yourself, ready yourself for a fresh coat of paint? Are you ready to see things in a different, brighter color? Blessings are the brushes dipped in the experiences of our lives, covering us with a touch from God, opening us up to limitless possibilities.

Blessing runs with gratitude. It's a relay race. The baton is handed to one another after every lap. They take turns, the focus for the moment being the one carrying the baton swiftly. Gratitude runs around the track and, before you know it, it's the blessing's turn. Blessing runs around the track and then, once again, it's gratitude's turn. These two runners depend on one thing: don't drop the baton.

Living a life of blessing is truly a lifestyle. Blessings are there; we just have to notice them. Remember—gratitude's power is, first and foremost, its ability to point out blessings. Blessing's power is, first and foremost, its eagerness to point to the One who blesses.

LIGHT

"I will love the light for it shows me the way, yet I will endure the darkness for it shows me the stars."

Oz Mandino

"Light is less something you see directly and more something by which you see all other things."

Richard Rohr

Twenty minutes into the cavern, the experiment began. It was a funny experiment, one which took place several times per day at this particular location. Pay the entrance fee, walk through a set of doors, and immediately feel the lumbering humidity, smell the dampness within the earthen clay. What you see, however, is dazzling. Pointy rock formations jutted from the ceiling and floor from years of tiny minerals deposited from ever-dripping waters. The stalagmites and stalactites formed a gnome-sized forest of brown, tan, orange, and other earth-tone colored, pine tree–shaped promontories. The sheer mystique of the underground world captured the gaze of all the paid visitors.

After gathering everyone a little closer to where he stood, the tour guide said a few words then walked fifty feet toward the left side of the cave and switched the lights off. And left them off, saying he wanted the darkness to have a moment to settle in. The tour guide, I'm sure, considered this experiment part of his routine as he led fascinated crowds periodically throughout the day. Possibly he invented the experiment to fight off the boredom and monotony of walking into this cavern six times a day. (To be fair, it is I who called what happened an "experiment." The tour guide would never do so for fear of liability, and the underwriters would frown upon that.)

As the darkness "settled," I found myself thinking of a cliche I once heard and held my hand in front of my face to see if it were, in fact, possible to do so and see nothing. My palm touched my nose, but I had no visual of a hand. My ears tingled, having just learned that other senses try to compensate when one particular sense is blocked. The utter blackness overwhelmed all those who walked this half an hour into the cavern. The tour guide proved himself right—we needed that moment to allow the darkness to envelop us. It didn't take long.

What happened next simply astounded us paid customers. The tour guide, standing a considerable distance away, lit a match. We heard it first. A cardboard box of tiny wooden sticks shaken as he fumbled one into his fingers. Then the sound of one abruptly scratching on sandpaper. Every eye rapidly zeroed in on that diminutive flicker burning on top of a tiny sliver of wood. Even from thirty feet away the flame almost hurt my eyes. *Wow.* But with that minuscule light, I was able to see the beautiful smiles, glowing eyes, and radiant faces of those around me. I saw people in a better light.

A vast, deep, cavernous darkness is powerless compared to the flame from a single matchstick.

The truth about darkness finds fertile ground in a far bigger arena than the center of a cave. Walking through the exit doors back into real life, back into the pressures of deadlines, the angst that sometimes comes with parenting, the fear of shootings, the constant newsfeeds of war, the smell of freshly disinfected hospital rooms, the sight of tears dripping from the eyes of someone at the table next to you, the flashing lights of twenty cars with a hearse leading the way, the harsh critics that somehow got in your ear—yes, a moment is all that is needed to let the darkness settle in.

Darkness, however, is not an all-powerful entity. It has a fatal flaw, a weakness so great that a tiny matchstick can defeat it. Darkness is utterly incapable of covering light. The only way for darkness to drape its cloak over any given space, shrouding everyone from using our primary sense of sight, is for that light to be snuffed out. The power of darkness, the fear it awakens, the insecurity it evokes, the path it blackens only falls on us in the absence of light. Light, on the other hand, intrinsically contains the power to rid a space entirely of darkness and its obscuring haze. Darkness flees at light. Never the other way around.

I lost my clutch one evening in a remote part of the eastern shore of Virginia. Sheer momentum allowed me to pull the car to an abandoned gravel parking lot, stopping us in front of a deserted motel, a relic from bygone days. All the windows were broken and curtains flapped as if waving to us in the warm winds. I took that as a warning sign and hastily walked my wife across the street and over to the gas station and convenience store. From there we sent a message to Uber through the app, to which they made clear that no Uber drivers could be found anywhere near. Great start. Apparently no tow trucks either, as we waited five and a half hours for a flatbed which arrived from a southern part of Maryland. At that point, we were just happy to see the yellow lights.

After retrieving the car, we climbed aboard the cab of the truck. It would be quite a long drive, so we struck up small talk. I asked the driver about his family, how he began driving tow trucks, what a typical day or night looks like for him, generating stories and a bit of laughter. (It is amazing what kind of situations people who need a tow get themselves into.) Somewhere in the dialogue, things turned to purpose and life and God. In the course of that, he indicated that he felt a higher purpose from above in what he does. When I asked what that higher purpose is, he said, "to make someone's day brighter when it just got a little darker."

Light overtakes darkness.

I awoke the other night, for no apparent reason, to large red digital numbers reading four thirty. Way too early. I turned over to the other side of my pillow in an effort to wish the clock away and sleep again, but my brain said, "way too late." So I lay there awake. Unfortunately, the gears begin when my eyes open. Darkness and weariness become the lubricants for worry, stress, and overthinking.

Sometimes you just want the night to be over. Minutes crawl when you watch the clock. I think Einstein was right—time warps. For me, especially at that time of night. If sleep is not an option, and climbing out of bed proves too cold, then I clamor for the promise of a new day.

And then I heard a chirp. Was that a bird? Or maybe a mattress spring? So I wait. And then another. And another. I am invited ever so slightly to that new day promise. Even birds sing a joyful song when a hint of light wakes them from the bushes. The window begins to glow an iridescent blue while the tree right outside takes shape. Then a faint, golden tone mixes on the palette of my yard and I am convinced—a new day, indeed. Arise. See brighter things. A little light is good, more is even better.

Light is, after all, hope. Most people wouldn't define it that way, choosing rather to speak of particles, rays, physics, and prisms. But I think light's greatest characteristic is hope. Hope to see a path on which to walk. Hope to read another page. Hope to begin a new day. Hope is most keenly visible when a spotlight shines on goodness, where once it was hidden in the thick smog of selfishness, hatred and violence.

In the recesses of my mind, I often use the two words "light" and "hope" synonymously, which is why I spent a considerable time deciding whether to title this chapter "light" or "hope." Eventually, I chose "light" due to the fact that it can be picked up by our sense of sight. We see it. We see what light does, offering to us a glimpse into the shape and color and beauty of our surroundings. Hope is not so much seen as it is felt. Hope is something we sense deep within based primarily on positive indicators. We determine a probable outcome because something we did *clicked*, something we noticed may bring events together, a rope with which to climb from the pit, a match to light a fire, an awning to keep you dry, a person to shield you from danger. But light shows you both things, from a rainbow made of the color spectrum all the way to the destination far in the distance where the gold pot rests. That is "light" and "hope."

I look at the vast darkness pouring from the cauldron of the internet's newsfeeds and wish the witch who stirs it to be gone. My wishing power eventually melts to the floor, leaving me in a puddle of my own anger, sadness, or tears. But then I remember the match in the cave, the stars against the black night sky, the hundred-thousand candle-power beacon revolving slowly upon a cylindrical tower on the cape.

Darkness runs away in the light of hope. It has no choice.

Light reminds us that goodness will one day win. Light tells us that justice climbs through the fog and lands on top of that red-and-white striped tower. Next time you decide to spend your evening at a movie theater, choose a movie where justice wins, the bad guy gets what they deserve, the superhero defeats the villain, the unexpected person becomes the person of the hour. As you walk out, look into people's eyes. Notice the expression on their faces. Peel your ear to hear some of the comments shared among the crowds walking back to their cars. There is a good reason why those movies make the most box office money. We crave hope that good will ultimately win the day.

This is also a good reason for the tradition of Christmas lights. I convinced myself a long time ago that the more Christmas lights, the better. It takes me a minimum of three hours to string 3500 little white lights onto our cut Christmas tree. The sparkle is spellbinding. Lights on the mantle. Lights weaved into swags hanging on the dining room chandelier. Lights wrapped around the garland over the doorframes. It's all a reminder.

I bring my family to distant neighborhoods to drive slowly by houses with tens of thousands of

LIGHT

lights. *They get it,* I think. I enjoy seeing how people light their homes, hearths, trees, bushes, windows, light posts. May they all see the purpose in the effort, and may all who see be reminded of the meaning of Light. Because there *is* light, and there *is* hope.

Light played a prominent role on the first Christmas. The serenity of the season, celebrated with nativities and manger scenes, creates charm and mystery. Light brought hope. The wise men followed a star. The shepherds gazed at the radiance of the singing angels. None compared to the light which laid in a manger. "The one who is the true light, who gives light to everyone, was coming into the world" (John 1:9).

The people were ready for this light because they yearned for hope. It was a long wait from the time Isaiah the prophet spelled out this hope, this light. Seven hundred years before the birth of Jesus, the prophet Isaiah took keen interest in this light-bearer. With the pending onslaught from the Assyrians, he told of a day when the nation of Israel would surely be ravaged. Slavery, poverty, and misery would indeed follow. That day, when it came, would dash hopes and embitter hearts. Desperation would be the dense fog hovering over the land. Darkness everywhere. And nothing else.

But the winds of Isaiah's words shifted favorably.

"Nevertheless, that time of darkness and despair will not go on forever... but there will be a time in the future when Galilee of the Gentiles, which lies along the road that was between the Jordan and the sea, will be filled with glory. The people who walk in darkness will see a great light. For those who live in a land of deep darkness, a light will shine" (Isaiah 9:1-2).

Darkness was coming, but hope was rising.

I find it interesting that Isaiah possessed the ability to describe this hope in any way possible, even to use the word "hope" itself to describe the future. Other words were at his disposal as well. Anticipation, or promise, or expectation, or confidence. As dynamic as those words are, they would not do. He used none of them. Only one word would suffice, one word that hemmed in all the other words, summarizing an indisputable hope: *light*.

If light is hope, then it is also freedom. What holds us back from greater things? What demoralizes us, rendering our soul unrecognizable? What controls our desires? What makes us downcast? What weeds choke color from our garden? What chattering hooves chase us? Why do we have to hide? Without freedom and light, we wander captive to the darkness. If hope does not show itself, we are relegated to keep asking those questions, to keep running and hiding while doing so.

But I have a request. Light the match, and then see how you might answer those questions.

I find it interesting that Jesus made it a point to heal the blind on numerous occasions. In the midst of the many stories of his miracles, blindness—just as it was prophesied about Jesus hundreds of years before—would be a specialty of his. "At that very time, Jesus cured many people of their diseases, illnesses, and evil spirits, and he restored sight to many who were blind" (Luke 7:21). The rarity of blindness among us today makes one wonder if blindness was indeed as prevalent in the first century as it seems upon reading of those healings, or maybe Jesus just wanted to make something very clear—that he is the light of the world, one whom darkness will never be able to snuff out. "...and his life brought light to everyone. The light shines in the darkness, and the darkness can never extinguish it" (John 1:4-5).

Even the blind, who live in darkness, will see the great light, and their sight will be restored because of it. Light and hope will break forth like the dawn, when darkness goes back into its corner, replaced with the light of an expectant future.

IN THE WIND

One such recorded healing of a blind man happened in Jericho, to a beggar named Bartimaeus. Blindness gave rise to a meager existence, and Bartimaeus's life was no exception. Left to beg, a blind man like him could only hope for a few coins with which to continue his daily routine. After arriving to the city gate by means of a walking stick, and possibly a family member, he would begin to call for help. A few coins, that's all. He can't see anyone walk by, only hear the footsteps of those walking to the market. Fleeting thoughts of ever regaining sight grew more sparse every day he sat on the ground, reliant upon generous crowds. After having leaned on the wall near the gate for so long, his back could speak to his location, as certain parts of the wall were built with different stones and less capable craftsmen.

Days turned into weeks, and weeks turned into months, and months to years. Lose hope, and you lose everything. He had to stay motivated. It was hard, pure and simple. He knew his hope was waning, but every day set his mind to do what he had to do to survive.

But wait, could this day be different? When one's eyesight diminishes, hearing amplifies. And what did he hear? That this Jesus—the rumored miracle-worker, prophet, teacher—walked the streets of Jericho this very day. And he would soon pass by.

So he started yelling to Jesus. Begging for mercy. This was his hope, maybe his last ditch effort to ever see again. His glassy white eyes looked straight ahead, while his ears did the work of discovering where Jesus walked along the road. And he was close. Bartimaeus yelled louder, his beard touching his chest every time he opened his mouth. The people tried to hush him. But to no avail. He shouted louder.

"When Jesus heard him, he stopped and said, 'Tell him to come here'" (Mark 10:49).

What? Really? Did the crowds hear Jesus correctly? Did Bartimaus's name really come from the lips of Jesus? Yes. This day was different.

"So they called the blind man. 'Cheer up,' they said. 'Come on, he's calling you!' Bartimaeus threw aside his coat, jumped up, and came to Jesus" (Mark 10:49-50).

Jesus stopped, approached Bartimaeus, then asked a simple question. "What do you want me to do for you?" (Mark 10:51).

"'My Rabbi,' the blind man said, 'I want to see!'" (Mark 10:51).

Light and hope. That was his request. Ours, too. Jesus wants everyone to know he offers exactly that.

"And Jesus said to him, 'Go, for your faith has healed you.' Instantly the man could see, and he followed Jesus down the road" (Mark 10:52). Wouldn't you?

I read this story recently and smiled. I love the emotion, the hope, the near-miss experienced by the blind man his whole life. But not today. Jesus called his name, and he saw the light.

Do you remember the story of the woman, the prostitute, who was to be stoned to death? Jesus removed her shame, guilt, and remorse. The crowds, having seen the response of the religious leaders, stayed to listen to what Jesus taught next. Jesus not only offered the woman forgiveness, but hope as well. This, too, was offered to all the onlookers.

Jesus continued to remind the people who he was, why he was here. "Jesus spoke to the people once more and said, 'I am the light of the world. If you follow me, you won't have to walk in darkness, because you will have the light that leads to life'" (John 8:12). That about sums it up. Hope lives. Just as physical light is necessary for physical life, so spiritual light is necessary for spiritual life. Jesus gives the light that leads to life because that is who he is. His light awakens something in our souls, convincing us that it's not all just a pipe dream. It's real.

What are the dark corners in your life? Where do you need light, hope? Do you feel yourself walking in what seems to be a land of darkness? Do hope and freedom seem to you to be an elusive pair, two butterflies worth chasing but never possible to catch?

There is hope. It is found in a matchstick, in seeing, in the stars, no matter how small, which shine in a canvas of blackness. When all is dark, we need light. In that moment when darkness begins its ominous advance, face the sun, moon and stars and let them remind you of who it is that truly gives light. There is a Light that will never be extinguished, and that darkness will never overtake. Hope is found there, in the One who *is* light.

LOVE

"The greatest happiness of life is the conviction that we are loved for ourselves, or rather, loved in spite of ourselves."

Victor Hugo

"Love makes your soul crawl out from its hiding place."

Zora Neale Hurston

I checked the gold leaf lettering on my ivory cardstock invitation one more time, making sure I wasn't late. The parking lot was nearly full—we jumped out of the car and walked as fast as possible across the greens in a race against the DJ, upon whose cue will start things off. We grabbed a seat just in time, and the processional began.

Beautiful bouquets of light blue and white matched the dresses chosen by the bride. The groom stood eagerly at the altar, awaiting the moment when his soon-to-be bride would walk the aisle. She was escorted slowly by her father, who at once took a seat. Then, side by side, words were spoken to the bride and groom by the minister, vows spoken to each other, and a kiss at the end. Everyone cheered as they walked back down the same aisle, hands in the air, this time as man and wife.

The wedding guests reunited under a large white tent following the idyllic outdoor wedding, the wedding party busy taking pictures. Caterers dressed in black and white strolled and mingled while holding trays of baby Reubens, crab-topped mushrooms, mini egg rolls, and perfectly cooked beef teriyaki on a long wooden stick. Already full from the appetizers, we were soon asked to make our way to the correct table. We fought the crowd hovering around the seating chart, then meandered to table eight. Small talk ensued and I noticed myself parched, mostly from the heat of the outdoor wedding. Iced tea and lemonade was self-serve in large glass containers on a counter at the far corner of the tent. My first thought after noticing my initial thirst was that my wife would also want a drink. She had just stepped out, so I was unable to ask her. Carrying two glasses of iced tea—hers mixed with lemonade, just the way she likes it—I spotted her at the other end walking toward me.

We spoke at the exact same time: "Hey, I got you some lemonade tea," and, "Hey, I got you some coffee with cream."

Turns out she got up from the table to get me some coffee, just the way I like it. We laughed. We caught eyes. And after these many years of marriage, we were reminded that we're still in love. I knew her well enough to know she loved salty appetizers and would need a cold drink on a hot day. She knew I would need caffeine after the long service (featuring what was surely the longest message from a minister in the history of this venue). So we just went and did. It's what love does.

A certain amount of complexity surrounds the true understanding of what love is. There are two reasons for this: first, the word itself, and second, the feeling. The word "love" has become as commonplace as any in the English language. We love birthday cake and we love Christmas. We love Hallmark movies and hosta growing by our sidewalk. We love staycations and swimming. We love ocean waves and nice watches. We love cookouts and fluffy clouds. We love our kids, our spouse, our cousins. We love God. Such a diverse word, with endless definitions.

But I like my definition best: I got her a glass of iced tea, she got me a cup of coffee.

Love is far more than merely preference, or admiration, or temporary excitement. When discussing our love for things, those words may apply. But when discussing our love for people, mere admiration falls very short. We understand what people mean when, after having unwrapped a gift, they say they love it. We all have developed the habit of using that word for such things, but for the purposes of this chapter, I would like to fixate the word love onto the subject of people—that deeper kind of love.

There is an unmistakable and indescribable love that washed over me when each of my three kids were born. It was a love that attached so immediately, so notably—a love which opened a new place in my heart, one I never knew I had. And from that moment, the love only grew more each day. Is that even possible? Yes. And it's miraculous. I love my kids more with each birthday. I love my kids more with each trip to the beach. Every football and basketball practice. Every flower show. Every graduation. Each new job they embark on. Every conversation over a home-cooked meal. I see the progress and I love. I see the struggles and I love. I love through hard conversations. Love through long walks. Love through an impromptu coffee or pizza. Who knew that our capacity for love could grow so much? I know a sliver of what God must feel for us, this God who loves us so perfectly. How do I describe this love? I feel it. I know it. Putting it into words, while fun to try, falls short. When we only have one word for love, it can be hard to properly discuss.

The ancient Greek language may be of assistance here. While the English language has one primary word for love, the Greeks had several, three of which are mentioned in the Bible. The first—*eros*. We sometimes call this kind of love "attraction" or "desire." It is the part of love which touches the mind and emotions at a level that draws intense interest. We like what we see or hear. We like what it feels like to be near that person. We desire that person and enjoy them, but don't fully care about their well being. Generally, it's in the category of initial attraction, like sparks flying when meeting someone you want to date. Taken to its extreme, it gives birth to lust. It is also a sustained attraction...so long as the magnetic pull doesn't diminish. Which is the problem with *eros*. It is susceptible to attrition because it's not plugged into a more permanent energy source. Prone to be fickle, temporary, and self-centered, *eros* can't fully be trusted.

There is a second word—*phileo*. We get words like philanthropy (doing good for others) and Philadelphia (city of brotherly love) from this root. *Phileo* gets us a little closer to the heart of true love. It is the love one has for family and friends. It is the kind of love displayed by best friends as each seeks the other's well-being and happiness. We do not have *phileo* toward enemies. There is a deeper affection, a genuine concern, a real desire to be nearer to a person when *phileo* is involved. *Phileo* differs from *eros* in that *phileo* more so gives, *eros* more so takes. *Phileo* shares commonality with *eros* in that both are tethered to the emotions. Both can be associated with familiar faces and strangers alike. Both motivate us to some sort of action. But the difference is in the depth. *Phileo* love moves far beyond initial acquaintance or attraction.

One more word describes yet another degree of love for the Greeks—*agape*. The previous two words prove insufficient for the task of defining a love that bores so deep, shows so much concern, acts so swiftly, as to call it divine. This *agape* type of love speaks of the noblest, deepest of all loves. It goes beyond feelings, yet is certainly felt. It goes beyond friendship, though characterizes the best that friendship has to offer. *Agape* is first and foremost active, willful, and delighted to be so. It resolves to put the welfare of others above our own, and finds the whole process joyful. *Phileo* cannot love enemies. *Agape* chooses to. *Agape* gives of self sacrificially and willingly. It is, in fact, the only word adequate to describe the love of God.

LOVE

A little bird distracted me while watching the wedding ceremony, turning my head toward the foliage of a springtime woods. I was happy for the bride and groom—the bride whom I knew since she was a child. I wondered where the years flew, how they had vanished so quickly, like that little bird. But my great wish and prayer for them was that their love flourishes—and not just *their* love, but the love of everyone sitting in the white folding chairs and everyone lined up in the front.

The minister said something that brought me back from birdwatching: "Marriage is not a 'give and take.' It is a 'give and give,' and a 'forgive and forgive.'"

That was profound. That's *agape*.

All of us yearn to be loved in a way that accepts us for who we are, the good, bad, and ugly. There is security in that, in the overlooking of faults, mistakes, and bad choices of our past. No one is immune from those things. To love anyone is to love that person for who he or she is, in spite of the past, the scars, the habits, and the nervous ticks. While all three loves have their place, it is *agape* that will show others the full extent of our love because it is active, self-sacrificial, and truly desires what is best for the other person, even if the best requires difficult conversations or tough choices.

The stark reality hits us in moments of honesty: sometimes we don't deserve to be loved in that way. We acted poorly—by choice—so how can we deserve love like that? *Agape* covers that and offers a love that goes beyond only what we hear, see, and know about someone, to the intrinsic value of the human being herself or himself. Which is what a man named Nicodemus needed.

Nicodemus was a prominent religious leader who knew much about religious law, punishments, and traditions. He was well-respected, but like many of the Pharisees, he failed to grasp the basics about how God works among his people. Pharisees experienced vast difficulties in getting past the rules. It seemed behaviorism (doing the thing required) replaced righteousness (doing the right thing for the right reasons) as the primary religious force. Walking by faith under the freedom of forgiveness seemed foreign to the religious leaders of the day. The fluster Nicodemus felt as to why and how Jesus performed miracles and taught with such authority, combined with the determination to stick to religious tradition at all costs, shrouded his view of Jesus of Nazareth. Nicodemus simply couldn't believe that Jesus was the long-awaited Messiah, God in the flesh.

Nicodemus was a Pharisee, part of a group of respected Jewish scholars who distinguished themselves with a strict observance of the Jewish laws. But he was also a member of the Sanhedrin, which was the religious judicial branch of the Jewish people. Being a Pharisee and member of the Sanhedrin, and one so knowledgeable of the prophets and their Messianic message, he sure asked a lot of questions. Intrigued, mystified, confused, and inquisitive, he finally got his chance with Jesus. And so the conversation—or inquisition—began.

Jesus answered question after question with responses that would grab the soul. The things Jesus said often motivated those nearby to stay and listen. Curiosity and intrigue are powerful tools to keep one pinned to a seat, ears open. It was no different with Nicodemus. Jesus talked of love, the *agape* kind. He talked of a God who is for the people, not against. A God who makes a way, not a roadblock. At one part of the conversation, Jesus said to Nicodemus words which would later become one of the most famous Bible verses in history.

"For God loved the world so much that he gave his one and only Son, so that everyone who believes in him will not perish but have eternal life. God sent his son into the world not to judge the world, but to save the world through him" (John 3:16-17).

Profound. Weighty. Compassion was not typically the first thing Pharisees would exhibit, nor attribute to God. No, this was different—a sacrificial love. Rescue love. Freedom love. Life-giving love. Flesh and blood love. God has really outdone himself this time.

Jesus's entire life demonstrated his insistence on seeing, feeling, and doing that which was in the other's best interest. He modeled it, then taught it. That was always Jesus's pattern. So, the night Jesus spent in that upper room—which proved to be his last before the crucifixion—he did both.

The disciples walked the dusty streets of Jerusalem's Mount Zion district, their feet coated with dirt, mud, and blood from a few cuts. The Jewish customs dictate that a servant would fill a bowl with water, drape a rag over their shoulder, kneel before the guest, and clean both feet. When they stopped for a time, the rabbi teacher Jesus, sitting among his closest friends, waited a moment to see if any were willing to begin the foot washing. None. No movement whatsoever toward a bowl, towel, or the water. Jesus saw this as another teaching opportunity and made it memorable. He rose from his seat and, at that very moment, transformed into a servant. He washed every one of the disciples' feet.

The disciples resisted at first, questioned this whole nonsensical picture, but ultimately succumbed to the gesture upon the insistence of their Rabbi Jesus. He seized the occasion, washed their feet, then instructed the disciples. After asking the disciples if they understood what he did and why, he made it crystal clear in order that they knew the correct answer.

"And since I, your Lord and Teacher, have washed your feet, you ought to wash each other's feet. I have given you an example to follow. Do as I have done to you" (John 13:14-15).

Jesus, once again, modeled and then taught. The action point? Do that for one another. Serve. Love that way. He capped that portion of the evening, just before the start of the meal, with his most important teaching of the night: "So now I am giving you a new commandment: Love each other. Just as I have loved you, you should love each other" (John 13:34).

Love each other. Love each other enough to serve one another, even when no one wants to. Love enough to honor the one across from you, even if you can't think of a reason. Love enough to put yourself second, even when you know you'll get dirty. The full extent of his love was yet to come. But this was a good start.

When the supper dishes were cleared, Jesus continued more of this intimate conversation with his disciples. Love dominated the rhetoric. The master, talking to his followers with authority, respect, and wisdom, said, "I have loved you even as the Father has loved me. Remain in my love" (John 15:9). It was an invitation to allow the *agape* love of Jesus to settle in on each disciple, a love that would never let them go. This perfect love from God has as its focus: people.

Jesus also hinted at the way he would finally show the extent of his love. "There is no greater love than to lay down one's life for one's friends" (John 15:13). It was lost on the disciples, though Jesus several times throughout his ministry warned of impending violence and his own tragic death. But what was not lost on the disciples was the genuine *agape* love Jesus showed, with perfect consistency, to every last one of them. It was his way. And it still is.

Seems that over time, more and more people had questions they wanted to ask Jesus. Many of the questions came from religious leaders trying to square Jesus's love for all people from every strata of life—regardless of religion, social prominence, financial status, gender, age, race—with his ability to perform miracles and with his insistence on being the Son of God. The religious experts inquired of Jesus to gain clarity, but at times tried to trap Jesus.

This was one such time.

With dark blue robes, white-and-blue headwear, tassels hanging from sleeves, and scrolls in hand, the group of Pharisees once again came to an impasse with Jesus. And once again, they devised a question that surely would be too hard to answer, or at least have no good answer. One man, well-studied and rehearsed in the law of Moses, stepped forward to ask the question of the day.

"Teacher, which is the most important commandment in the law of Moses?" (Matt. 22:36).

I think that to be a very difficult question. After all, the Law and the Prophets (basically the entire Old Testament) contain thousands of commandments. How can anyone say one is more important? Who has the authority to rank them? Who even has that kind of wisdom?

But the question was no match for Jesus. He went right to a concept that no one could argue: love. "Jesus replied, "'You must love the Lord your God with all your heart, all your soul, and all your mind.' This is the first and greatest commandment.

A second is equally important: 'Love your neighbor as yourself.' The entire law and all the demands of the prophets are based on these two commandments" (Matt. 22:37-40).

Love for God, who can argue that? Love your neighbor, who would disagree with that? So it seems, love outdoes all—love for God and love for those around you. Now the Pharisees were speechless. It was a good answer, and a surprise to them that Jesus had an answer at all. One of them even complimented Jesus on such an answer.

We were made to love. Yes, we have to choose to do so, but it is *why* we were made. Love originated with God. God initiates love. God gives us the ability and opportunity to show his love. I have seen love when a mother wraps a gift for her sixteen-year-old. I have seen love when a stranger hands a homeless woman a blanket and lunch. I have seen love when someone answers their phone to hear, "I'm sorry" on the other end. I have seen love when someone pays a surprise visit to help rid fleas from a friend's apartment. I have seen love on the beach when two octogenarians unfold two worn aluminum chairs just to sit and hold hands while watching the waves.

When I reached out to take a cup of coffee offered by gentle hands, I saw love. And it looked a lot like God.

FINDINGS

"The three grand essentials of happiness are: something to do, someone to love, and something to hope for."

Alexander Chalmers

"Truly successful decision-making relies on a balance between deliberate and instinctive thinking."

Malcolm Gladwell

A neighbor's recently acquired puppy decided to take a chance on a screen door that didn't latch. Its nose pushed the white frame just enough for it to squeeze through and dash away, disappearing among the cookie-cutter homes. Nothing evokes more tears among children than a runaway puppy. Tears gush, and the search party begins. That's always the order. Once the kids start crying, something has to be said and a specific action has to be taken, even if you feel it's in vain. No one wants to be a bad parent. So the sobbing kids call for Mom, and Mom comes running to hear the story. Big Brother and Sister, having heard the news, dash out the same screen door…and the hunt is on.

The quest for the runaway puppy begins with a frantic calling of the poor little four-legged creature's name. That coincides with a walk through the neighborhood asking pedestrians and gardeners and joggers if they perchance saw a puppy run by. They scour the yards, look through the white lattice below backyard decks, peer behind trees—all the while, calling.

If the effort thus far proves fruitless, the hunt moves to the next phase, which is knocking on doors. So they split up, ring doorbells, knock on storm doors, talk to the homeowners, and run to the next house like it's Trick-or-Treat time. An hour goes by like a minute. Nothing yet, except more crying. Time for step three: Dad gets a call at work. He leaves early, and on the way home drives around the neighborhood at ten miles per hour for an hour and forty-five minutes.

Still nothing.

But the search can't stop. Too much love. It was decided to reconvene at the dinner table. Time for step four: photocopies tacked onto telephone poles. And to top it off, those same photocopied papers get taped to road signs and piled in stacks at the pharmacy and other kind-hearted establishments (who can say no to a crying kid and a lost puppy?). And then the social media blitz—moms' groups, H.O.A., friends, neighbors, sports teams, garage sale groups. The quest for the lost puppy becomes a monumental effort, all driven by love, compassion, and a deep desire to be near the furry little friend once again.

God is doing that for you. Did you know that? He calls, seeks, draws, posts, and sends messages, driven by a love and compassion for you that won't quit. Maybe it's not pictures on a telephone pole, but it is specific nonetheless. He sends a rainbow, prompts a question, gives you purpose, fills a void, heals a broken heart, forgives a wrong, notices your pain, provides a ray of hope, causes things to work together, covers you with love. It's a monumental effort.

As seen in the previous chapters, many were drawn to Jesus. His love, compassion, power, wisdom, and desire for people to know God gathered people naturally. It was a grassroots movement, and before long, hundreds were following him from town to town. To some, this was the best thing going—time well spent. His teaching was helpful, demonstrated love, and had the power to change people. But the things he said weren't always easy to hear. Sometimes his words hit a little too close to home.

On one particular occasion, Jesus spoke plainly about the need to come to God, and to allow him to help them come to God. After all, that was Jesus's purpose. Some didn't like that and had their own idea of religion and God. One by one, some of the people sauntered away. Jesus, seeing the dissipating crowd and feeling the rejection, asked his disciples a question, the nature of which revealed the extent to which the mass exodus pained him.

"Then Jesus turned to the twelve and asked, 'Are you also going to leave?'" (John 6:67).

A good question. One which the disciples, I'm sure, considered for themselves, especially after having seen so many others leave. But they followed Jesus this far, experiencing what it was like to be near to the Son of God. His teaching, his miracles, his compassion for the poor—all of it followed them as well, molding them into people that looked more like their master every day.

The question lingered only for moments before Peter stepped forward with an answer. His response flowed downstream through the recesses of his logic and memory. His answer was sensible, yet simple: "Lord, to whom would we go?" (John 6:68).

Another good question. Peter's profound observation revealed a severe truth: there is no other option. In other words, Jesus's goodness is too good to leave. He saw it. He heard it. He felt it. He knew it. Jesus had the words to live by in this life and the life to come.

Peter followed that question with a rationale for asking it, saying, "You have the words of eternal life. We believe, and we know you are the Holy One of God" (John 6:67-68).

I want to stop here for a moment. What about that? Eternal life? What about our mortality? What about death? It is one thing all of us will face. But no one, not even myself, really wants to talk about it. I admit that to be a sobering thought, even a sorrowful one. All of us know people who died, people whom we wish were still here. We hope they are in a better place—I feel that. I also feel that I want something more than wishful thinking or hoping when it comes to the death of someone I love—and, for that matter, my own.

My mom loved local history. Wherever she lived, and subsequently where I lived, she gathered what information was made available through the chamber of commerce, historical society, or other similar private organizations. When that wasn't available, she would walk through graveyards. As a kid in tow, I followed and listened as she read bits and pieces of history etched on the stones. The tall, thin, marble stones from the 1700s, barely legible, recounted occupations, family members, even cause of death, and always age. Latter stones used granite—these were more resilient to weather and erosion, but contained much less information.

A life tells a story. Every life. And so I always thought it good that markers rested in the grass, telling those who pass by of that person's significance, no matter who they were or what they did for a living.

Cemeteries, at least once or twice, ought to make us think that far ahead. I am not advocating dwelling on our own mortality. I am suggesting, however, that mortality—the thought of something beyond this life—is yet another way God gets our attention. But everything in us wants to avoid thinking about it. So we ignore it. We come up with a few phrases that make us and everyone around us feel a little better. We try to beat aging and even death, holding back that tide with health, medicine and stress-free living as much as possible. One thing with tides, though: you can't stop them.

Sometimes we even try to create heaven here on earth, thinking that maybe this is all there is.

Maybe dying ends everything. I think that would be a rather sad existence, if that were true.

Jesus, having been tried and found guilty in a joke of a courtroom, was sentenced to death. Nails, the size of railroad spikes, were driven ruthlessly into his hands and feet. He was left, hanging on a cross, to die.

Two others were crucified that day, criminals who had a fair trial and were found guilty. These two nameless men—one on the left, and one on the right of Jesus—committed crimes and received their due punishment. Jesus committed no crime, but after an absurd mockery of a trial, was sentenced to death anyway. There they hung, crowds gathered around, soldiers waiting, agony afflicting Jesus and the two criminals. The pain, unbearable, was just too much. But before the three of them died, they shared a short, pained conversation.

"One of the criminals hanging beside him scoffed, 'So you're the Messiah, are you? Prove it by saving yourself—and us, too, while you're at it!' But the other criminal protested, 'Don't you fear God even when you have been sentenced to die? We deserve to die for our crimes, but this man hasn't done anything wrong'" (Luke 23:40-41).

There comes a time when all of us have to think through our own life, all our adventures, achievements, and mistakes. It's not a bad thing. Just hard. Both of the criminals pressed in on thoughts of their past, their life, their mortality, and their God for good reason—they would be dead before nightfall. The second criminal, however, made a solemn request after seeing clearly the reality of the situation.

"Jesus, remember me when you come into your Kingdom" (Luke 23:42).

What else could he do, where else could he go? Jesus responded with grace and hope, as he always does.

"And Jesus replied, 'I assure you, today you will be with me in paradise'" (Luke 23:43).

Assurance. Hope. Not just for this life, but for the life to come. Not just wishful thinking, not just pithy sayings. Real hope. "Today, you will be with me…"

I saw a lady through a plate glass window as I sat eating lunch in town. Finishing a cup of coffee, my writing having slid into a rut, I stood to refill the mustard-colored ceramic mug. I recognized her lovely gray hair as I peered out the window, holding a full mug of hazelnut coffee. I stepped out for a moment onto the sidewalk, waved, and walked over to say hello. She was a friend whom I knew had a blessed life, God watching over her. But her life hadn't always been easy. She smiled, told me her tax man was supposed to meet her, then looked silently into my eyes. Her eyes filled with mist.

"Things seem a little darker these days," she said, her voice quivering. "But you know what? The darker it gets, the brighter the light."

"Yes. No doubt," I responded.

"But I always remind myself of two questions," she said. "Do you want to hear them?"

"Please."

"What's the worst thing that has ever happened in this world?" She paused. "Jesus hung on a cross."

I nodded my head.

"And now, what's the best thing that has ever happened in this world?" She paused again. "Jesus hung on a cross."

I stared for a minute. How profound. She reached out to give me a hug and told me to be blessed. I watched my feet walk to the car.

She is right. This wonderful, mysterious, kind, forgiving, bright, benevolent, and loving man was tortured and executed to die a death he did not deserve—to pay a penalty *I* deserved. He died to pay for our sins, for my sins. Death to the Son of

God, life to me. It hardly makes sense. But that is the wonder and mystery of God. That is powerful light and love from another place.

Hush. Let me tell you a secret: death did not have the last word. Not then. Not ever. The grave, as it turns out, was only a temporary shelter, not a permanent resting place. The heavy stone which sealed the opening of this tomb rolled away, revealing the startling fact: it was empty. But how? No body was laying in the tomb. But where had it gone? Joy mixed with fear. But why? Because of *agape*. Because he has your best interest in mind. Because he knows that a living God will be more precious to you, more necessary, more fulfilling than anything else.

"O death, where is your victory? O death, where is your sting?" (I Cor. 15:55)

I love rhetorical questions. The power in a rhetorical question lies in the immediacy at which the answer comes to us, with no need of further explanation, and with no expectation of a verbal response. Just sheer rumination, the kind that touches the heart.

"He gives us victory over sin and death through our Lord Jesus Christ" (I Cor. 15:56).

Jesus himself said, "There is more than enough room in my Father's home. If this were not so, would I have told you that I am going to prepare a place for you? When everything is ready, I will come and get you..." (John 14:2-3). That is the assurance we have. Period.

Jesus asked another thought-provoking question in a time well before his death. Once again, multitudes had gathered to hear words from Jesus in hopes of mending broken pieces, soothing deeper wounds, securing a better future, and growing with God. Calling his disciples together, Jesus expressed his concern for the beautiful crowds, the thousands of people who sat before him—they had no dinner, and no means to acquire it.

"I don't want to send them away hungry, or they will faint along the way," Jesus said. The disciples replied, "Where would we get enough food here in the wilderness for such a huge crowd?" (Matt. 15:32-33).

It was merely a setup. Jesus asked, "How much bread do you have?" They replied, "Seven loaves and a few small fish."

That's all he needed. That day, Jesus fed estimates of over 8,000 people. It's just like Jesus to care for the minutiae of our daily lives, to worry about us skipping a single meal. And it's just like Jesus to take what little we have to offer and do something amazing with it. Our "only" is what Jesus uses to bring blessing and goodness to the people he dearly loves.

When he sent the people home, Jesus hopped into a boat to row to the other side of the lake. The disciples followed. This seclusion gave Jesus the opportunity to debrief the miraculous feeding of the crowds, leading to the question at hand. He asked them, "Who do people say that the Son of Man is?" (Matt. 16:13).

Fair question. Stories about Jesus abounded. Opinions about Jesus proliferated the landscape, providing volumes of subject matter for debate. "Well," they replied, "some say John the Baptist, some say Elijah, and others say Jeremiah or one of the other prophets."

Then he asked them, "But who do you say I am?" (Matt. 16:14-15).

It's one thing to answer on behalf of others—pretty easy, really. Avoid the risk of sharing your own opinion and slide right out of the conversation. But answering such a direct request is a different thing altogether. Jesus primed the pump with the first question, and water flowed with the second.

Peter drank it in and responded boldly. "You are the Messiah, the Son of the Living God" (Matt.

16:16). Jesus not only 'blessed' Peter after hearing his response, he projected a special future for him: the church would begin with Peter as a foundational rock.

And now the question comes to us. Like stepping to the plate, ready to face a ball being launched from a pitcher's hand at a hundred miles an hour, choice and courage are etched into the label of the bat. With those two things, we will swing. Choice opens doors and courage allows us to walk through them. Especially with life-altering decisions. God has so much more in store for you.

Several years ago, I was asked to be a guest speaker at a prison for juvenile offenders. I spoke with a young prisoner while in the recreation area of that particular detention center. We talked about many things—family, interests, skills, what got him here, faith. He told me he did not believe in God. I asked why. He said because he couldn't see him. I get that. I asked him to look out the window and recount to me what he saw.

"Trees."

"Yes, and what are the trees doing?"

"Blowing around."

"How are they blowing around?"

"Wind."

"Wind? I don't see any wind."

"Look at the trees."

"I see the trees. I just don't see the wind."

"But..."

"We don't *see* the wind, we only see what wind does."

We stood silent for a moment. Then he laughed and said, "I get it."

For so many, seeing is believing. But flip the script, and believing is seeing. The point is, we can't see God. But we see what he does. The effects are evident. One of the things which Jesus does today is stand at a door—the door to your heart—and knock. The thing about belief is you have to invite him in. Accepting him is merely receiving the love, forgiveness, and newness that Jesus offers. It's saying two simple things: "Yes, Jesus," and, "Thank you, Jesus."

Once he comes in, he stays for good. Nothing you say, do, or think can run him out—not that you'd want to! Once you live in the mystery of belief and wonder, there's no going back. Letting him in means grabbing hold of the purpose for your life. It means filling the emptiness, healing the pain, dealing with remorse, and living under his blessing of light and love. It means becoming a whole person, having the spiritual part of you satisfied and fulfilled. It means grasping the 'something more.' And it's all offered to you.

And by the way, it worked. The searching and calling proved successful. They found the little dog, safe and sound, its little tail wagging. Someone drove the lost puppy to their house. There was much laughter and crying of happy tears—a true celebration. It was a monumental effort.

"The wind blows where it wishes, and you hear the sound of it, but cannot tell where it comes from and where it goes."

John 3:8

"Be still and know that I am God."

Psalm 46:10

ACKNOWLEDGEMENTS

We are all interconnected in some way. No truer than compiling a manuscript which turns into a book. Publishers, editors, creative teams, support behind the scenes and, of course, you as readers all play a part. So I want to first start with you. Thank you! Thank you for choosing to enter into a little of my life, and mine yours as you explore the bigger work that God is doing in you.

Second, I want to thank the people at SPS. Everything over there is done with excellence. They have an abhorrence for cutting corners. I would like to give a special thank you and shout out to Brett Hilker at SPS for so patiently and painstakingly leading me through this process in a very expedited amount of time. Thanks, Brett, for always having time for my questions and a smile to go along with it.

I also want to give a huge thank you to my editor, Christina Bagni at Wandering Words Media, who has exceptional gifts with words and an uncanny ability to make narrative flow like it should. She got behind my book and it is better because of her. Thank you, Christina!

A special thanks to Shaun Nestor, my assistant at church and aspiring writer, who gave hours of thought and time with me. He supplied brainpower when I got stuck, and humbly played a behind-the-scenes role to get this through the finish line. Thanks man!

A huge thank you to my wife, Kimberly, and my kids, Harrison and his wife Taylor, Garrett, and Elyse for encouragement, brainstorming, and wisdom when I needed it most.

And, for sure, "thank you" goes to Jesus, who promised to be with me always, good times and bad, and makes good on that promise every day.

NOW IT'S YOUR TURN

Discover the EXACT 3-step blueprint you need to become a bestselling author in as little as 3 months.

Self-Publishing School helped me, and now I want them to help you with this FREE resource to begin outlining your book! Even if you're busy, bad at writing, or don't know where to start, you CAN write a bestseller and build your best life. With tools and experience across a variety of niches and professions, Self-Publishing School is the <u>only</u> resource you need to take your book to the finish line!

DON'T WAIT

Say "YES" to becoming a bestseller:

https://self-publishingschool.com/friend/
Follow the steps on the page to get a FREE resource to get started on your book and unlock a discount to get started with Self-Publishing School

ABOUT THE AUTHOR

Rev. Dr. Billy Burch (D.Min., M.Div., M.A.) is the Lead Pastor at Christ Community Church in West Chester, Pennsylvania, where he has served in ministry for 30 years. Billy holds a Doctor of Ministry degree (Rawlings School of Theology, L.U.) and is passionate about connecting with people and helping them to experience Jesus in a meaningful way. He also holds a Master of Divinity and Master of Arts in Youth Ministry (Trinity Evangelical Divinity School). Billy and his wife live in Downingtown, Pennsylvania and have one daughter, two sons, one daughter-in-law, and two grandchildren. Spending time with his wife and kids is his favorite thing. In his free time, he can often be found snowboarding, jet skiing, rejuvenating at the beach, and following Baltimore sports teams.

Visit his website at billyburch.com. You can also find Billy on the *At the Table* podcast, *Everything Jesus* podcast, and the *[UN]apologetic* podcast wherever you stream your podcasts.

Can You Help?

Thank You For Reading My Book!

I really appreciate all of your feedback, and I love hearing what you have to say.

I need your input to make the next version of this book and my future books better.

Please leave me an honest review on Amazon letting me know what you thought of the book.

Thanks so much!

Billy Burch

Made in United States
Orlando, FL
13 May 2024